# UNBREAKABLE

## JAMES J. HOLDEN

### WITH ADESSA HOLDEN

# UNBREAKABLE
Copyright © 2024 Mantour Ministries

All rights reserved. No portion of this book may be reproduced, stored in a retrieval system, or transmitted in any form or by any means—electronic, mechanical, photocopy, recording, scanning, or other—except for brief quotations in reviews or articles without the prior written permission of the author.

Published by 4One Ministries, Inc. Visit www.mantourministries.com for more information on bulk discounts and special promotions, or e-mail your questions to info@4oneministries.org.

All Scripture quotations, unless otherwise indicated, are taken from the The ESV® Bible (The Holy Bible, English Standard Version®). ESV® Text Edition: 2016. Copyright © 2001 by Crossway, a publishing ministry of Good News Publishers.

The Holy Bible, New International Version®, NIV®. Copyright ©1973, 1978, 1984, 2011 by Biblica, Inc.™ Used by permission of Zondervan. All rights reserved worldwide. www.zondervan.com The "NIV" and "New International Version" are trademarks registered in the United States Patent and Trademark Office by Biblica, Inc.™

Scripture quotations from THE MESSAGE. Copyright © by Eugene H. Peterson 1993, 1994, 1995, 1996, 2000, 2001, 2002. Used by permission of NavPress. All rights reserved. Represented by Tyndale House Publishers, Inc.

Scripture quotations marked (NLT) are taken from the Holy Bible, New Living Translation, copyright © 1996, 2004, 2007 by Tyndale House Foundation. Used by permission of Tyndale House Publishers, Inc., Carol Stream, Illinois 60188. All Scripture taken from the New Century Version®. Copyright © 2005 by Thomas Nelson. Used by permission. All rights reserved.

Design: James J. Holden


Subject Headings:
1. Christian life 2. Men's Ministry 3. Spiritual Growth

ISBN 978-1-965809-00-6
ISBN 978-1-965809-01-3 (ebook)
Printed in the United States of America

# DEDICATION

I want to dedicate this book to all the men who wake up and fight to be free daily. Instead of running from their sins and struggles, they work to overcome them and gain victory. In turn, they set a model for other men to follow. These men have the heart of an unbreakable man and inspire me to follow their example daily.

# TABLE OF CONTENTS

1. GET OFF THE MAT! — 7
2. THE THIRD MAN — 15
3. CHOOSING SIDES — 25
4. GETTING OFF THE MERRY-GO-ROUND — 33
5. THE BIGGIE — 43
6. THE SECRET TO SUCCESS — 55
7. SHHH…IT'S A SECRET — 67
8. THAT'S NOT HOW WE ALWAYS DID IT — 85
9. BATTLE SCARS — 101
10. MONEY MAKES THE WORLD GO AROUND — 113
11. ONE MORE ROUND — 123

PERSONAL NOTE FROM JAMIE — 131

WORKBOOK — 133

BIBLIOGRAPHY — 157

# CHAPTER ONE
## GET OFF THE MAT!

The light show is over. The weigh-in is complete. *"Let's Get Ready To Rumble!"* has been proclaimed. The time for smack talk has ended. It's just two men face-to-face in the ring. The goal is to break the other man, knock him out, and be the last man standing. You want to be the one with his hand raised in the air, standing over your opponent sprawled out on the mat. The man who has proven one thing.

He is the Champion.

He is unbreakable!

Over history, many men have entered the warrior's ring and emerged victorious.

- Tyson
- Ali

- Foreman
- Holyfield
- Marciano
- Frazier

These are not just names. They are the embodiment of triumph. They are the men who have conquered the ultimate battle, emerging as the unbreakable man, the World Heavyweight Champion. Their victories are a testament to the power of resilience and determination.

For decades, we have been regaled with movies of the great unbreakable Rocky Balboa. The movie franchise has grossed $792,052,221 at the box office,[1] as people have watched time and time again the story of a man who refused to get knocked down. People love to see an unbreakable man.

Anyone who knows me knows I am a huge fan of Rocky. I have seen the *Rocky* movies so many times I can almost quote them. My favorite is *Rocky III*, but the most impressive fight is *Rocky IV,* when Rocky beats the Russian giant, Ivan Drago.

Imagine my joy when I saw the trailer for *Creed II*. I loved the first *Creed* movie! I loved seeing Rocky transition from the unbreakable warrior to the coach, teaching Apollo Creed's son, Donnie, to fight.

I was so excited to hear there would be a *Creed II*. Then they dropped the trailer. The opening clip shows Adonis getting knocked out cold and falling to the mat. Then, it shows him in a hospital, beaten, bruised, and broken. The rest of the trailer is Rocky talking, telling Donnie not to take the fight. Rocky even references Donnie's dad, Apollo, dying in his arms. Where was this movie going?

Then you see it. Donnie's opponent in the ring, back turned, with one word on the back of his robe.

DRAGO!

I. FREAKED. OUT.

I watched the trailer about thirty times. I couldn't wait to see this movie, and it did not disappoint.

In the movie, Donnie ignores Rocky's advice and takes a fight against the son of the man who killed his father. As Rocky warned, the fight is a disaster. Donnie gets destroyed by Viktor Drago. He gets beaten so severely that he is in the hospital for weeks. But worse than the physical beating, the fight leaves Donnie a broken man.

He is mentally destroyed. He can't fight. He can't find his way back into the ring. He appears to be down for the count.

> ★★★★★★★★★★★★★
> IF YOU WANT TO CHANGE THINGS IN A BIG WAY, YOU NEED TO MAKE SOME BIG CHANGES.
> ★★★★★★★★★★★★★

Then something beautiful happens. Rocky comes back and makes Donnie face his fears. He makes him see what is going on. Then, he offers a helping hand to help him up off the mental, defeated mat Donnie is living on.

What follows is one of the most incredible training montages in film history. Rocky knows that if Donnie is going to beat Drago in a rematch, he has to become unbreakable. So he takes him to the desert to a fight camp where fighters go to start over. In the words of Rocky, *"If you want to change things in a big way, you need to make some big changes."*[2]

I love that line! Too many broken men never get unbroken because they keep going down the same path, make the same choices, and fall into the same sinful patterns. They stay broken because they don't do the work necessary to change. They do the same things, hoping for different results, but all that ends up happening is they get knocked on their butts again.

Creed had to make big changes. He had to learn to take a beating. He had to get tough. His core had to be strengthened. He had to learn to endure, to never give up or stop fighting. Defeat was no longer an option. No matter how hard the punch, he had to stand. When he got knocked down, he had to get back up and fight again.

Finally, Donnie entered the ring for a second time with Drago. This time, he was a different man. He took a beating from Viktor again, but this time, he stayed in the fight.

Drago landed a mass punch on Donnie at the end of the fight, and Creed went down hard. It looked like the fight was over. But then something glorious happened.

Instead of staying down, we see Donnie slam his glove on the mat. He still has fight in him! He punches the mat over and over again. He is down, but he is not out!

Slowly, in agony, he rises to his feet, ready to fight again. And fight, he does. He goes after Drago like a possessed man.

As he fights back, the fight play-by-play guy says a line that I absolutely love. He says, *"There is no way around Viktor Drago. He has to go through him."*[2]

Go through him he did! In the end, Donnie won the fight and was once again the champion, but even more, he was now an unbreakable man.

Guys, it is time to get up off the mat and get back into the fight! You cannot keep living broken and defeated! Victory is there for you. Through God, you are unbreakable!

Yet, many men seem to struggle to fulfill their destiny as an unbreakable man.

It has broken my heart over the past few years to see so many men of God be broken and lying on the mat, with the enemy standing in triumph over them.

- Pastors leave their churches after falling into sin.

- Husbands lose their marriages because they are defeated by temptation.

- Finances are in ruin because men are broken under the burden of debt.

- Reputations are destroyed because of lives lived in secret and deceit.

The list goes on and on.

The world is filled with too many broken, defeated men. It is time to get off the mat and get back in the fight.

★★★★★★★★★★★★★
THERE IS NO WAY AROUND THE ENEMY STANDING IN FRONT OF YOU. YOU HAVE TO GO THROUGH IT!
YOU HAVE TO FACE IT, FIGHT IT, AND DEFEAT IT ONCE AND FOR ALL.
★★★★★★★★★★★★★

It is not God's will for His men to live broken, defeated lives. He ordained for His children to be victorious.

God is calling His men to get back into the fight.

No man has to stay broken and defeated. There is hope!

But as the announcer said, there is no way around the enemy standing in front of you. You have to go through it!

You have to face it, fight it, and defeat it once and for all. The good news is that victory is already promised if you get back up and fight!

> *But thanks be to God, who gives us the victory through our Lord Jesus Christ. -1 Corinthians 15:57 (ESV)*

Victory is guaranteed, and God promises to be present with you in the fight!

> *For the Lord your God is he who goes with you to fight for you against your enemies, to give you the victory. Deuteronomy 20:4 (ESV)*

However, you can't fight lying on the mat. You have to punch the mat, get back up, and fight.

This book is designed to help you become an unbreakable man. It was born out of a moment in the Word months ago.

I woke up to my Alexa blaring some obnoxious song to wake me up. I sat up and slowly turned my body to put my feet on the floor (you don't want to move too fast at my age in the morning; wait, younger guys, you'll understand soon enough), and picked up my phone.

I checked my email and clicked on the *Mantour Ministries Daily Bible Plan* link to read the Word (I'm not just the author of the Bible plan, I'm also a client.)

The daily reading was in 2 Kings. I had read this passage many times before, but today, it jumped off the page, grabbed my face, and said, **"Look at me!"**

Ok, it really didn't do that, but it sure felt like it.

As I read it, the Holy Spirit said to me, *"This is why so many of My men are being defeated. It keeps them laid out on the mat, knocked out, and unable to get back to their feet to gain victory. This is what I want you to write about in this book."*

This came as quite a surprise to me because I already had not just one but two different outlines written for this book. I did the first one in the Fall of 2023, but over time, it became apparent that it wasn't what I was supposed to write, so I trashed it and wrote another outline. For the next four or five months, I planned on that being the book for 2025. However, I had this nagging feeling that this wasn't it either.

Then God spoke to me as my sleep-crusted eyes read this passage in 2 Kings. I talked to my sister about it, and she instantly said, *"That will be such a better book than what you had planned."*

This is that book. As you work through it, my desire is for you to gain victory over the things that have knocked you down over and over and kept you from moving forward with God.

Men, I am tired of seeing broken men never reaching their full potential as men of God, and I want to help you leave the ranks of the beaten and enter the ranks of the victorious. Are you ready to start again, to get back in the fight, and become an unbreakable man? If so, let's get started.

*Note: Each chapter will have group study questions so you can work through them with a group of men. I STRONGLY encourage you to do this. We have been blown away by the testimonies of how God has worked through these books as men worked through them together in their men's ministry. There is strength in numbers. Work together with other men and choose to ride or die together. The book also includes a workbook so you can go more in-depth personally and also be a format for discussion in your small group.*

**UNBREAKABLE**

## Group Study Questions

1. What is your favorite *Rocky* movie?

2. Why do men struggle to get off the mat and gain victory? Why do you?

3. What struggle is constantly beating you down?

4. What have you tried to do to get victory?

5. This chapter quoted Rocky saying, *"If you want to change things in a big way, you need to make some big changes."* Are you willing to make big changes?

6. What does the word *"UNBREAKABLE"* mean to you?

7. After reading this chapter, what is one thing you will put into practice or one thing you will change in your life?

8. How can we, as a group, help you do this?

# CHAPTER TWO
## THE THIRD MAN

My favorite Rocky movie is *Rocky III*. I have watched it so many times that I can pretty much quote it. One of my chief goals in life and ministry is to be a man who never loses the *"Eye of the Tiger."*

If you've never seen this movie, first of all, what is wrong with you?!? But if you haven't seen it, it takes place after Rocky fights Apollo Creed for the second time and becomes the World Heavyweight Champion.

Immediately, his life changes. Rocky and Adrian go from being poor and struggling to a life of wealth and luxury.

The movie shows Rocky going through some title defenses against inferior opponents he can beat pretty handily. It shows him spending money, driving fancy cars, being on the cover of magazines, and all the things that come with fame and fortune. Meanwhile, parallel to all these clips, it shows a new boxer, Clubber Lang, played by Mr. T., training, working hard, and having an attitude while he struggles to get what Rocky already has.

Eventually, Rocky and Clubber Lang have a confrontation at the ceremony dedicating the Rocky statue in Philadelphia. Rocky announces that he is going to retire from boxing, and Clubber Lang explodes with anger that he won't get to fight Rocky. After a heated argument, Rocky declares he will do one last fight against Clubber.

Rocky goes back into training…sort of. He goes through the motions but isn't committed to training how he needs to train to win. He isn't retired and walking away from a battle, but he isn't exactly the fighting machine he used to be. He is just going through the motions, acting like a fighter but training like he's retired. And as you would expect, this half-hearted approach to fighting ends with him being knocked out cold and lying on the mat.

It wasn't until Rocky committed to the hard work of boxing… training, sparring, building endurance…that he could fight Clubber and win.

Like Rocky, we often find ourselves thinking we are stuck between two paths. In Christianity, things are often seen as black and white. You are either a fighter serving God or living a life of sin as an unsaved man. However, there is a third option.

God showed me this third option that morning as I read the daily reading in 2 Kings. Let's look at the passage.

> *In the fifty-second year of Azariah king of Judah, Pekah the son of Remaliah began to reign over Israel in Samaria, and he reigned twenty years. And he did what was evil in the sight of the Lord. He did not depart from the sins of Jeroboam the son of Nebat, which he made Israel to sin.*

> *In the days of Pekah king of Israel, Tiglath-pileser king of Assyria came and captured Ijon, Abel-beth-maacah, Janoah, Kedesh, Hazor, Gilead, and Galilee, all the land of Naphtali, and he carried the people captive to Assyria. Then Hoshea the son of Elah made a conspiracy against Pekah the son of Remaliah and struck him down and put him to death and reigned in his place, in the twentieth year of Jotham the son of Uzziah....*
>
> *In the second year of Pekah the son of Remaliah, king of Israel, Jotham the son of Uzziah, king of Judah, began to reign. He was twenty-five years old when he began to reign, and he reigned sixteen years in Jerusalem. His mother's name was Jerusha the daughter of Zadok. And he did what was right in the eyes of the Lord, according to all that his father Uzziah had done. Nevertheless, the high places were not removed. The people still sacrificed and made offerings on the high places. He built the upper gate of the house of the Lord. -2 Kings 15:27-30 & 32–35 (ESV)*

This passage contains a lot to unpack. To do this, I want to focus on three different men. Two are named here, and one is implied. These three men are vital to understanding the truth of this book.

**1. The Man Who Follows God Wholeheartedly**

The first man we need to discuss is the implied man, King David. King David was the second king of Israel. He was the gold standard against which all the following kings would be measured. Don't believe me? Check this out.

> *For when Solomon was old his wives turned away his heart after other gods, and his heart was not wholly true to the Lord his God, as was the heart of David his father. For Solomon went after Ashtoreth the goddess of*

*the Sidonians, and after Milcom the abomination of the Ammonites. So Solomon did what was evil in the sight of the Lord* **and did not wholly follow the Lord, as David his father had done.** *Then Solomon built a high place for Chemosh the abomination of Moab, and for Molech the abomination of the Ammonites, on the mountain east of Jerusalem.* -1 Kings 11:4-7 (ESV)

*Asa began to reign over Judah, and he reigned forty-one years in Jerusalem. His mother's name was Maacah the daughter of Abishalom. And* **Asa did what was right in the eyes of the Lord, as David his father had done.** -1 Kings 15:9-11 (ESV)

*Amaziah the son of Joash, king of Judah, began to reign. He was twenty-five years old when he began to reign, and he reigned twenty-nine years in Jerusalem. … And he did what was right in the eyes of the Lord,* **yet not like David his father.** -2 Kings 14:1-3 (ESV)

This small sample shows how all the other kings were compared to David. David loved God and lived every day trying to follow and obey God and serve Him only. He wasn't perfect, but his heart was committed to following God, and he always strived to do things God's way and according to God's commands. When he sinned, he would repent and turn to God. He was indeed the *"man after God's own heart." (Acts 13:22)*

I love that title. I WANT THAT TITLE! I want to be a man who is so committed to God that my life revolves around serving Him and pleasing Him. This type of man is the man who refuses to get knocked down and stays down. He gets back up and fights another round!

## 2. The Man Who Doesn't Care About God

The second time of man is the man we see at the beginning of our original passage. Let's look at him again.

> *In the fifty-second year of Azariah king of Judah, Pekah the son of Remaliah began to reign over Israel in Samaria, and he reigned twenty years. And he did what was evil in the sight of the Lord. He did not depart from the sins of Jeroboam the son of Nebat, which he made Israel to sin.*
> *-2 Kings 15:27-28 (ESV)*

King Pekah was an evil man who didn't even attempt to follow God. He lived a life of sin, leading his people into idol worship. The nation ended up being taken captive by Assyria, all because they rejected God and didn't follow His ways.

The second type of man here is an unsaved man. He isn't following God or trying to live for God. His sinful nature controls him. He is pursuing the world and all it offers without thinking of God.

So we have seen two types of men: a saved man who serves God wholeheartedly, rejecting the world and its high places and serving God with hunger and passion, and an unsaved man who doesn't consider God at all. In the *"church world,"* we often focus on these two men, saved and unsaved. We talk about the two paths, the straight and narrow and the wide path. But there is a third man we have to look at.

## 3. The Man Who Follows God But Doesn't Tear Down The High Places

The third man is a man who loves God but doesn't go all the way for God. We see this in the life of Jotham.

*In the second year of Pekah the son of Remaliah, king of Israel, Jotham the son of Uzziah, king of Judah, began to reign. He was twenty-five years old when he began to reign, and he reigned sixteen years in Jerusalem. His mother's name was Jerusha the daughter of Zadok. And he did what was right in the eyes of the Lord, according to all that his father Uzziah had done.* **Nevertheless, the high places were not removed.** *The people still sacrificed and made offerings on the high places…In those days the Lord began to send Rezin the king of Syria and Pekah the son of Remaliah against Judah. Jotham slept with his fathers and was buried with his fathers in the city of David his father, and Ahaz his son reigned in his place. -2 Kings 15:32-35 & 37-38 (ESV)*

Jotham was a good king who served God, but he didn't tear down the high places. As a result, he didn't get the gold star seal of approval as a man who followed in David's ways. Instead, we read that he and his kingdom faced attacks from Syria because he didn't tear down the high places.

As we look in the Old Testament, we see this is a problem with many of the Kings of Israel and Judah.

- King Asa (1 Kings 15:11,14)
- King Jehoshaphat (1 Kings 22:43)
- King Jehoash (2 Kings 12:2-3)
- King Amaziah (2 Kings 14:3-4)
- King Azariah (2 Kings 15:3-4)

These kings fell into the trap of the third man. They served God but didn't tear down the high places.

They don't choose the path of the world, altogether rejecting God, but they also don't choose the narrow path of wholeheartedly serving God. Instead, they walk a treacherous, unclear path full of high grass, stumps, holes, and traps.

The third man cannot be unbreakable if he doesn't tear down his high places. They love God, but they only go halfway with Him. However, it's the halfway that kills us!

> ★★★★★★★★★★★★
> THE THIRD MAN LOVES GOD, BUT THEY ONLY GO HALFWAY WITH HIM. HOWEVER, IT'S THE HALFWAY THAT KILLS US!
> ★★★★★★★★★★★★

Not going all the way with God and removing the high places in our lives will always result in us being laid out on the mat, struggling to get to our feet. It keeps us defeated, always struggling, and honestly, always upset with God that He isn't just making our lives easier and better. But God can't bless us when we want God on our terms while holding on to our comfortable, hidden, high places.

Notice that it says, *"the Lord began to send Rezin the king of Syria and Pekah the son of Remaliah against Judah."*

Why would God send these attacks?

> ★★★★★★★★★★★★
> GOD ALLOWS US TO SUFFER FROM OUR HIDDEN HIGH PLACES, HOPING THAT THE SUFFERING WILL CAUSE US TO RIP THEM DOWN AND FOLLOW HIM COMPLETELY.
>
> ★★★★★★★★★★★★

He did it because He loved them and wanted them to realize the sin they were committing. He wanted them to realize that they weren't following Him wholeheartedly, that they were allowing the world's system of worship to mingle with how God wanted them to serve Him, turn in repentance, and start new.

This is why God allows us to suffer the consequences of not following Him wholeheartedly. He allows us to suffer from our hidden high places, hoping that the suffering will cause us to rip them down and follow Him completely.

Which man do you want to be?

It would seem obvious to me that if you are reading this book, you won't fall into the category of the second man discussed, a man with no desire to follow God. But I don't want to make that assumption. Maybe you are someone in a prison, rehab center, or halfway house who was given this book. Maybe a friend gave it to you. Maybe your wife made you attend a Mantour Conference, and you won this book in our drawing. Perhaps you found it in your rehab facility library. If you are a man who has never made that first commitment to follow God, I encourage you to do it NOW.

God loves you. He sent His only Son, Jesus, to die on the cross in your place. Jesus was punished for your crimes! But He did it so that you could be forgiven by God and have a relationship with Him. He died, then rose again, defeating sin, death, and hell, freeing you to leave the path of the second man and turn and follow God wholeheartedly. If that is you, pray this prayer right now and accept Christ as your Savior.

*Heavenly Father,*

*I come to You in the name of Jesus, seeking Your forgiveness and grace. I acknowledge that I have sinned and fallen short of Your glory. I believe that Jesus Christ, Your Son, died on the cross for my sins and rose again, offering me the gift of eternal life.*

*Today, I turn from my old ways and ask You to cleanse my heart. I invite Jesus to come into my life, to be my Lord and Savior. I surrender my will to Yours, trusting in Your love and mercy.*

*Fill me with Your Holy Spirit, and help me to walk in Your truth and righteousness. Thank You for saving me, for making me a new creation in Christ.*

*In Jesus' name, I pray. Amen.*

If you prayed this prayer, congratulations! You are no longer the second type of man who is not part of God's family! I encourage you to tell someone at your church, or if in prison, your chaplain, about this decision. Find and read a Bible to learn more about God and your new life. Start with the book of John.

Now, for those of us who have been walking with Jesus for a while, it's time to ask ourselves: *"Have I been following God wholeheartedly like David, or am I content living a half-hearted commitment to God, constantly being defeated by your high places?"*

If you have been living a defeated life, are you ready to get off the mat, fight back, and gain victory?

I encourage you to make it your mission in life to adopt the heart of David, who lived daily with a hunger and passion for God.

This means we want all of God that we can get.

We keep short accounts of our stumbles and immediately repent and start again.

A man with a heart like David doesn't stay on the mat… he gets up and fights on.

A man like David fights for freedom and gains victory. He is an unbreakable man!

This is my heart's desire and my decision for my life. Now is the time to choose: Do you want to stay defeated or live in victory?

**UNBREAKABLE**

# Group Study Questions

1. Who was a better bad guy, Clubber Lang or Ivan Drago?

2. What were the three types of men we discussed in this chapter?

3. Which type of man are you? Be honest with yourself.

4. Why is it so important to recognize and remove our *"high places?"*

5. This chapter stated, *"God allows us to suffer the consequences of not following Him wholeheartedly. He allows us to suffer from our hidden high places, hoping that the suffering will cause us to rip them down and follow Him completely."* How does this passage make you feel?

6. What changes do you need to make to follow God wholeheartedly like David?

7. After reading this chapter, what is one thing you will put into practice or one thing you will change in your life?

8. How can we, as a group, help you do this?

# CHAPTER THREE
## CHOOSING SIDES

Why do I like *Rocky* movies so much? One reason is that the *Rocky* movies show overcoming, perseverance, grit, and dedication. They have heart. They have intensity. They are motivating. When Rocky is getting beaten and battered in the ring, you just wait to hear that trumpet start playing, and you know he will get back on his feet and fight on to victory. It makes you want to run through a wall!

Rocky movies also always have great quotes. Don't believe me? Check out this year's *Unbreakable Daily Bible Plan*, and you will see what I mean.

One of Rocky's best quotes comes from the last Rocky movie in which we see Rocky put on gloves, *Rocky Balboa*. In the scene, Rocky's son Robert, played by Jess from the *Gilmore Girls* (I spent many years living with my mom and sister), is upset at Rocky's decision to fight again. But it's not really what he is upset about. He is upset that his life isn't going how he wants. Instead of taking responsibility for his life, he instead blames it on being overshadowed by his famous father. This is when we get one of the best quotes from any *Rocky* movie.

*"The world ain't all sunshine and rainbows. It is a very mean and nasty place and it will beat you to your knees and keep you there permanently if you let it. You, me, or nobody is gonna hit as hard as life. But it ain't how hard you hit; it's about how hard you can get hit, and keep moving forward. How much you can take, and keep moving forward. That's how winning is done.*

*Now, if you know what you're worth, then go out and get what you're worth. But ya gotta be willing to take the hits, and not pointing fingers saying you ain't where you are because of him, or her, or anybody.*

*Cowards do that and that ain't you. You're better than that!"*[1]

Great men issue great challenges to those around them facing a tough road ahead. This is one of Rocky's best. I even have a shirt with part of this quote on it.

In the Bible, Joshua once gave a Rocky-esque speech to the nation of Israel. He'd come to the end of the road. Joshua, born into slavery in Egypt, witnessed the plagues, lived through the Passover, and marched out of Egypt proudly when God set His people free.

He was Moses' aide and one of twelve spies sent to see the Promised Land. Before that task was over, he was one of two who said, *"We can do it—God has given us this land."* (Another Rocky-like speech, but not the one I want to focus on in this chapter.) Even though he was bold and courageous, he still had to endure forty years of wandering in the wilderness because of the ten spies and the people who cowered in fear.

After Moses died, he became Israel's leader. Following God's call to be *"strong and courageous,"* he led the people in the wars that defeated their enemies and led them into the Promised Land. He saw the walls of Jericho Fall, presided over Achan's trial (more on this later), watched the sun stand still, and defeated the kings of Canaan. I wonder if he thought, *"I can't believe this day is finally here,"* as he went through the task of dividing each area among the different tribes of Israel.

Joshua had lived an extraordinary life.

But, like all men, he was coming to the end of his journey. Before he died, he had one last task—one last challenge—to present to the people of Israel.

> *Joshua gathered all the tribes of Israel to Shechem and summoned the elders, the heads, the judges, and the officers of Israel. And they presented themselves before God. -Joshua 24:1 (ESV)*

With everyone gathered around him, he recounted all he'd seen God do for Israel throughout his life. Then, he issued this challenge:

> *Now therefore fear the Lord and serve him in sincerity and in faithfulness.*
>
> *Put away the gods that your fathers served beyond the River and in Egypt, and serve the Lord.*
>
> *And if it is evil in your eyes to serve the Lord, choose this day whom you will serve, whether the gods your fathers served in the region beyond the River, or the gods of the Amorites in whose land you dwell.*
>
> *But as for me and my house, we will serve the Lord. -Joshua 24:14-15 (ESV)*

This speech definitely needed the Rocky trumpet music playing as Joshua spoke! It was an iconic moment. Like a crowd of fans listening to a rousing speech from their favorite football coach, the crowd went wild.

"We're with you! We'll never turn back! Just like you, we will serve the Lord!"

But Joshua knew there was more to keeping this commitment than just cheering with a passionate crowd. If we continue to read Joshua 24, we see him say that:

> **But Joshua said to the people, "You are not able to serve the Lord, for he is a holy God He is a jealous God; he will not forgive your transgressions or your sins. If you forsake the Lord and serve foreign gods, then he will turn and do you harm and consume you, after having done you good." -Joshua 24:19-20 (ESV)**

Still, the people said again: *"We got this."* (Okay, they didn't exactly say that, but it fits.)

One more time, Joshua challenged them, and they said, we want to serve the Lord.

This is where Joshua's speech fits into the theme of this book: tearing down high places. It's when Joshua gives them the real challenge: Prove it.

> **He said, "Then put away the foreign gods that are among you, and incline your heart to the Lord, the God of Israel." -Joshua 24:23 (ESV)**

The surrounding nations had many gods they could choose to follow. They could serve Baal, build their Ashtoreth poles, or go to the temples of the prostitutes. No one was forcing them to serve God because of all that He had done for them. They were free to choose. We, too, have this same freedom.

There are lots of gods in our culture we can choose to serve. We can serve the god of power. We can dedicate our lives to the god of success. The god of pleasure is a choice many people enjoy serving. Sexuality can be our god of choice. Our world is surrounded by millions of gods that can replace serving God. We can choose these gods; however, they can come with a price. You can serve them, but you will be a broken and defeated man. Joshua knew the price and made his choice. We must make the same choice today…God or the world?

Because here's the thing: if you want to be an unbreakable man of God, it isn't enough to say, *"I want to serve the Lord"* when you're in church or at a men's event. It's a great start, but the real challenge comes when you return home and choose to serve God with all your heart and obey His commandments.

In our daily lives, we must choose to obey God's ways rather than the ways of the world around us.

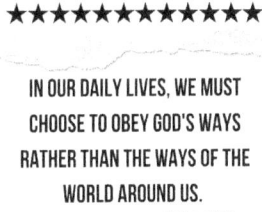

**IN OUR DAILY LIVES, WE MUST CHOOSE TO OBEY GOD'S WAYS RATHER THAN THE WAYS OF THE WORLD AROUND US.**

As men of God, we are called to do more than make this decision for ourselves. We are responsible for following Joshua's example and leading our families in making this decision.

You see, it's one thing to say, ***"As for me and my house, we will serve the Lord,"*** but do we actually do it?

- When push comes to shove, are we the first to prioritize prayer and Bible reading?

- Do we lead family devotions or complain that it means missing the football game?

- Do you keep your kids involved in church and church activities or leave it to your wife? Does she have to fight you if there's a sports/church conflict, or can she depend on you for leadership?
- Do you make tithing a priority or complain about it?
- Do you turn off the television when something inappropriate is on or wait for the kids to go to bed and watch it?
- Are you teaching your sons how a godly man treats women and showing your daughters what to expect from a godly man?

Because here's the thing—it doesn't matter how much you're involved in church, if you have a title or position, how much you raise your hands and dance around during worship or shout *"Amen"* during the sermon.

Who are you when you go home?

Straight talk: Growing up in the church, I knew far too many men who put on a show in front of the church people every week, but behind the scenes, they were addicted to porn, abusing their wives and their kids, and committing idolatry by excusing their sinful behaviors and choosing them over God's ways.

These men were the loudest in the crowd, but they didn't have the muscle it takes to accept the challenge, wholeheartedly serve God, and humbly lead their families to follow Christ.

While these men could put on quite a show, their families and lives were broken behind the scenes. Perhaps it's because they didn't fully understand what Joshua was trying to teach the Israelites: serving God isn't easy. It takes more than words. The commitment doesn't end at the altar. It starts there.

It continues when you go home and when you get up the next day.

- When hard times come.

- When other options are more appealing.

- When you have to deal with pain from your past.

- When you have to forgive.

- When you need to change.

- When it's time to sacrifice and put others first, to put on love, compassion, and kindness, and yes, once and for all, destroy the idols in your life.

It's a daily, weekly, monthly, yearly, lifetime commitment to serve the Lord.

If you want to be an unbreakable man of God, you must make and keep this commitment. It becomes your life's mantra —*as for me and my house, we will serve the Lord.*

> ★★★★★★★★★★★★
> IF YOU WANT TO BE AN UNBREAKABLE MAN OF GOD, YOU MUST MAKE AND KEEP THIS COMMITMENT. IT BECOMES YOUR LIFE'S MANTRA—AS FOR ME AND MY HOUSE, WE WILL SERVE THE LORD.
> ★★★★★★★★★★★★

Israel said they were committed to this, but as we saw in the last chapter and will see as we move forward, they really weren't. When push came to shove, they pursued the sins and customs of the world around them. As a result, they ended up broken and defeated.

My hope for all of God's men is we avoid these sins of the Israelites and pursue God wholeheartedly. But as Joshua said, we have to choose who we will serve. What is your choice? Will you serve the world and all it offers, or will you serve the Lord?

## Group Study Questions

1. What is your favorite Rocky quote?

2. Why is it so hard to reject the world and serve God in our daily lives?

3. What does it really mean to say that you and your house will serve the Lord?

4. Will you serve the world and all it offers, or will you serve the Lord? Honestly think about this choice and decide.

5. Why is it so important for an unbreakable man to make this decision?

6. After reading this chapter, what is one thing you will put into practice or one thing you will change in your life?

7. How can we, as a group, help you do this?

# CHAPTER FOUR
## GETTING OFF THE MERRY-GO-ROUND

One thing I have noticed in *Rocky* movies is that defeat often occurs when fighters don't take their opponents seriously.

Apollo Creed ignored all of Duke's warnings in *Rocky II*.

Rocky didn't take his fight with Clubber Lang seriously in *Rocky III*

In *Rocky IV*, Apollo Creed dies in the ring, surrounded by showgirls, James Brown, and an entire orchestrated show because he doesn't take Drago seriously. Over and over, fighters faced defeat because they didn't train or focus properly.

Men of God, we must take our battle seriously. We cannot allow complacency, tolerance of sin, or the world to defeat us. This is not how an unbreakable man acts or lives. As Apollo Creed said to Rocky in *Rocky III*, we need that *"eye of the tiger"* not just to fight, but win.[1]

In the last chapter, we read about the nation of Israel responding to Joshua's challenge to reject the nations around them and serve the Lord. Why was Joshua worried about this in the first place?

Because the nation of Israel had already started down the slippery slope of defeat. God had ordered the nation of Israel to go and defeat the people of Canaan and destroy them. I know this sounds harsh in today's world, but God did it for a reason. He knew if they didn't destroy the enemy completely, eventually, the enemy would destroy them. But Israel disobeyed God, and they didn't destroy the Canaanites. Let's rewind a bit in the book of Joshua to see what I mean.

> *Yet the people of Israel did not drive out the Geshurites or the Maacathites, but Geshur and Maacath dwell in the midst of Israel to this day. -Joshua 13:13 (ESV)*
>
> *But the Jebusites, the inhabitants of Jerusalem, the people of Judah could not drive out, so the Jebusites dwell with the people of Judah at Jerusalem to this day. -Joshua 15:63 (ESV)*
>
> *They did not drive out the Canaanites who lived in Gezer, so the Canaanites have lived in the midst of Ephraim to this day but have been made to do forced labor. -Joshua 16:10 (ESV)*
>
> *Yet the people of Manasseh could not take possession of those cities, but the Canaanites persisted in dwelling in that land. Now when the people of Israel grew strong, they put the Canaanites to forced labor, but did not utterly drive them out. -Joshua 17:12-13 (ESV)*

Israel tolerated the enemy among them. They don't destroy them or drive them out as commanded. Because of this, they opened themselves up to attack and defeat.

It only got worse after Joshua's death. Judges 1 tells us that after Joshua died, the tribes continued to fight but also continued tolerating the people of the land. This didn't fly with God.

> *Now the angel of the Lord went up from Gilgal to Bochim. And he said, "I brought you up from Egypt and brought you into the land that I swore to give to your fathers. I said, 'I will never break my covenant with you, and you shall make no covenant with the inhabitants of this land; you shall break down their altars.'*
>
> *But you have not obeyed my voice. What is this you have done?*
>
> *So now I say, I will not drive them out before you, but they shall become thorns in your sides, and their gods shall be a snare to you."*
>
> *As soon as the angel of the Lord spoke these words to all the people of Israel, the people lifted up their voices and wept. And they called the name of that place Bochim. And they sacrificed there to the Lord. -Judges 2:1-5 (ESV)*

You would think this warning would have shaken the people back into reality, causing them to destroy all their enemies and follow God wholeheartedly, as they promised God and Joshua. But they didn't.

> *And the people of Israel did what was evil in the sight of the Lord and served the Baals. And they abandoned the Lord, the God of their fathers, who had brought them out of the land of Egypt. They went after other gods, from among the gods of the peoples who were around them,*

> *and bowed down to them. And they provoked the Lord to anger. They abandoned the Lord and served the Baals and the Ashtaroth. So the anger of the Lord was kindled against Israel, and he gave them over to plunderers, who plundered them. And he sold them into the hand of their surrounding enemies, so that they could no longer withstand their enemies. Whenever they marched out, the hand of the Lord was against them for harm, as the Lord had warned, and as the Lord had sworn to them. And they were in terrible distress. -Judges 2:11-15 (ESV)*

In exact opposition to the vow made to Joshua, the people rejected God and followed the ways of the nations around them. They followed the gods of Baal and Ashtoreth, which included vile human sacrifice and disgusting sexual perversion. As a result, God had to judge them. They became defeated and in bondage.

*"Wow Jamie, isn't it harsh of God to judge them like this?"*

Not at all. God is both a holy and loving God. He must always do whatever He must to make us uncomfortable enough to turn to Him. However, He is also a loving and graceful God.

> *Whenever the Lord raised up judges for them, the Lord was with the judge, and he saved them from the hand of their enemies all the days of the judge. For the Lord was moved to pity by their groaning because of those who afflicted and oppressed them. But whenever the judge died, they turned back and were more corrupt than their fathers, going after other gods, serving them and bowing down to them. They did not drop any of their practices or their stubborn ways. -Judges 2:18-19 (ESV)*

## GETTING OFF THE MERRY-GO-ROUND

God's heart was always for the people to love and serve Him, and He constantly reached out to them to abandon their sins and turn back to Him. The entire book of Judges is a book of a cycle.

- Israel rejects God for the idols around them.
- God judges them.
- Israel cries out for help.
- God sends a judge to rescue them.
- The people served God until the judge died.
- The people reject God for the idols around them.

On and on the circle goes.

The people tolerated the sin and evil around them and didn't defeat it. Then, they started compromising and following the ways of the foreign nations. Finally, they rebel against God and His ways and embrace the ways of the world around them.

Before long, they are trapped, lying on the mat, beaten and abused. They could have escaped this cycle at any time if they had accepted God's grace and mercy, left the sin behind, and returned to following God wholeheartedly. But they kept falling back into the sinful pattern because they didn't take it seriously; they never fought it and destroyed it.

*"This is all interesting, Jamie, but what does it have to do with me?"*

We need to understand an important fact. God's plan was never for the surrounding countries to influence the nation of Israel. He wanted His way and His worship to reign supreme in the nation.

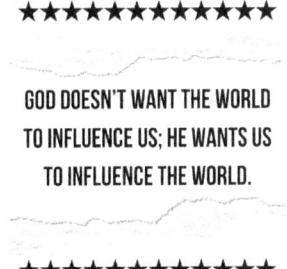

**GOD DOESN'T WANT THE WORLD TO INFLUENCE US; HE WANTS US TO INFLUENCE THE WORLD.**

Men, God doesn't want the world to

influence us; He wants us to influence the world. Why does it always end up the other way around? Why are Christians falling into sin instead of standing like a bright light, shining for God in a dark world?

Why are so many men of God knocked out and on the mat? Because, like the nation of Israel, they laid down and tolerated the sin and compromise. They didn't fight to victory; they settled for tolerance.

We aren't facing battles against Baal or Ashteroth and worshipping these pagan idols. However, we have sins, struggles, and trials constantly knocking men down and cycles we get trapped in and continue repeating. If we want to gain victory and become unbreakable, we must break this cycle of defeat and overcome it.

Men, we must do what the Israelites weren't willing to do…fight and win. Guys, we must show our sin no mercy. We must choose to fight for our freedom!

We need a William Wallace moment. Remember the scene in *Braveheart?*

Standing in a line, an army of ragtag fighters carrying their makeshift weapons is ready to fight for their beloved Scotland, but more importantly, for their freedom.

That is until they see the enemy.

Walking boldly in formation, clad in body armor, carrying swords and spears, the sight of the enemy makes them quake in their shoes. Completely intimidated and afraid, the amateur army begins to retreat.

That's when William Wallace appears on the scene and makes his famous speech, including these lines:

*"You have come to fight as free men, and free men you are. What would you do without freedom? Will you fight?"*

Then, a veteran soldier says: *"Fight? Against that? No, we will run; and we will live."*

To which Wallace replies: *"Aye, fight and you may die. Run and you'll live -- at least a while. And dying in your beds many years from now, would you be willing to trade all the days from this day to that for one chance, just one chance to come back here and tell our enemies that they may take our lives, but they'll never take our freedom!!!"* [2]

Like Israel, the army was intimidated and didn't want to fight and obtain victory. And yet, fighting is the only way to become an unbreakable man of God.

Men, we have two choices in life.

We can choose not to fight. We can choose to continue being oppressed by influences from our old ways of life, trapped in sin, heartache, and pain. You won't have to remember things you don't want to or face hard truths. You'll never see inside a counselor's office or spend hours journaling about your feelings.

But I wonder if those who make that choice someday don't look back on their lives and say, *"I wonder what could have been if I'd let the Holy Spirit do everything He wanted to do in my life? What if I'd been brave enough to let Him blow my mind, tear down every stronghold, remove every sin, and make me into everything He wanted me to be?"*

I personally don't want to wake up five, ten, or twenty years from now and think, *"What could God have done with my life if I'd been courageous enough to fight the battle in my mind and overcome it? Who would I be? How would my relationships be different? What would have happened if I'd been strong enough to fight?"*

I choose in my heart to fight for freedom, to not tolerate the sin trying to take my heart captive. Because as William Wallace said, *"What is more valuable than freedom?"*[2]

Freedom from sin, freedom from addiction, freedom from heartache and trauma—it's all worth the price, the risk, and the battle.

Perhaps today, you are standing in your own line of decision. The Holy Spirit is calling you to face your past or even the sins of your present and fight a spiritual battle to gain your freedom.

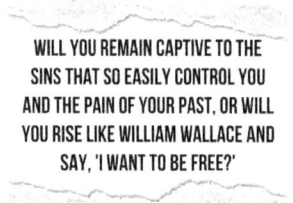
WILL YOU REMAIN CAPTIVE TO THE SINS THAT SO EASILY CONTROL YOU AND THE PAIN OF YOUR PAST, OR WILL YOU RISE LIKE WILLIAM WALLACE AND SAY, 'I WANT TO BE FREE?'

The choice is up to you. Will you remain captive to the sins that so easily control you and the pain of your past, or will you rise like William Wallace and say, *"I want to be free?"*

Will you follow Israel's path and tolerate the sin, allowing it to take control of your life and defeat you eventually, or will you have your Braveheart moment, wear your spiritual armor, and cry, *"Freedom!"*

There is only one choice for an unbreakable man of God.

## *Group Study Questions*

1. Why is it so important to remove complacency from our lives?

2. Did the Holy Spirit reveal any areas in your life where you tolerate sin or complacency?

3. How did you respond to the Holy Spirit's revealing of this sin? What actions did you take?

4. This chapter stated, *"God doesn't want the world to influence us; He wants us to influence the world."* Why does it always seem to end up the other way around? Why are Christians falling into sin instead of standing like a bright light, shining for God in a dark world?

5. Will you remain captive to the sins that so easily control you and the pain of your past, or will you rise like William Wallace and say, *"I want to be free?"*

6. After reading this chapter, what is one thing you will put into practice or one thing you will change in your life?

7. How can we, as a group, help you do this?

# CHAPTER FIVE
## THE BIGGIE

Have you ever played the *Madden* video game? I used to love this game. I would play it for hours in my younger, more carefree days. It was so much fun, and I became good at it.

The funny thing about *Madden* is that there are so many plays in the playbook that you can use, but often, a player has one or two favorites that always work for them, and they use them over and over.

If you are playing as the Tennessee Titans or now the Baltimore Ravens, you do a middle dive with Derrick Henry…unstoppable. A quarterback scramble by vintage Michael Vick was a guaranteed touchdown.

I always played with the Broncos, and there was a shotgun play I constantly used, *Gun Empty Trey Stick N Nod.* The four receivers ran go routes, clearing the middle of the field. The tight end would run a jag slant where he faked right and then slanted left. It was a sure first down every time I played it. If my opponent had just played a spy over the center of the field, it wouldn't have worked, but rarely did they adjust their style of play, and I'd constantly get the completion. I returned to it repeatedly because I knew it would always work and help me defeat the opponent.

Our enemy has a playbook he uses to defeat men of God. It is full of traps and schemes to knock us out. But he uses one particular play when nothing else works that repeatedly trips up men of God. If we will be unbreakable men, we need to understand that this is the enemy's play, identify it, and stop falling victim to it.

What is the play? Sexual sin, including pornography.

The enemy has been using this play since the early days of civilization. Often, we wonder why the Israelites were so dumb to always follow the ways of the Canaanites and other heathen nations around them, leaving them trapped, defeated, and separated from God. One answer is that they were attracted to the sex. What do I mean? Let's look at the Bible to find out.

We already discussed how Israel was ordered to go in and take possession of the Promised Land in Joshua. However, this was the second time they were given the order. The first time came during Moses's time, and Israel started conquering the land. However, sometimes, God would tell them not to fight certain kingdoms. One such time is found in Deuteronomy 2:9.

> *And the Lord said to me {Moses}, "Do not harass Moab or contend with them in battle, for I will not give you any of their land for a possession, because I have given Ar to the people of Lot for a possession."*

The people of Israel were forbidden to attack or harm Moab. However, the king of Moab did not know this. Because he was afraid of Israel and its military might, Balak, the king of Moab, hired

Balaam, a prophet, to come and proclaim a curse on the nation of Israel. The entire story is told in Numbers 22-25, but I will summarize for the sake of time.

When Balaam received the king's request and the offer of a huge financial windfall, he first said *"no."* However, a promise of money and wealth eventually made him make the trip. As Balaam proceeded on the long trek to Moab, he was stopped and warned not to curse Israel. This is done through the miraculous phenomenon of having his donkey speak to him. (It's a really cool story! I'll resist the many obvious jokes!) He was told that if he insisted on going, he may only say what God told him to say.

When Balaam arrived, he went to view the Israelites' camp and tried to speak his curse, but God only allowed him to bless the Israelites. Balak, furious at Balaam's blessing, demanded he try again.

The same thing happened each time he tried to curse Israel. Unable to curse them, Balaam decided to tell Barak what to do to trap Israel. He knew Barak couldn't defeat them. The only way they would be defeated was if they defeated themselves.

Revelations 2:14 tells us Balaam's sinister advice.

> *...you have some there who hold the teaching of Balaam, who taught Balak to put a stumbling block before the sons of Israel, so that they might eat food sacrificed to idols and practice sexual immorality. (ESV)*

Get the Israelites to serve false gods, and you'd get God to defeat them for you! The biggest enticement to serve the false gods around them was that so much of the worship of these gods included sexual sin and perversion. The worship involved sex, rape, prostitution (both male and female), homosexuality, any and every sexual perversion. There was something to tempt and trap everyone.

Balaam knew that the only way Moab could defeat Israel was if Israel turned on God, causing God to discipline them. Did it work?

> *While Israel lived in Shittim, the people began to whore with the daughters of Moab. These invited the people to the sacrifices of their gods, and the people ate and bowed down to their gods. So Israel yoked himself to Baal of Peor. And the anger of the Lord was kindled against Israel. -Numbers 25:1-3 (ESV)*

Like the Eagles tush-push at the goal line, it worked like a charm! The Moabite women seduced the Israelite men and caused them to participate in the sensual Moabite religious system. The Israelite men fell into their trap. As a result, God's anger fell.

> *And the Lord said to Moses, "Take all the chiefs of the people and hang them in the sun before the Lord, that the fierce anger of the Lord may turn away from Israel." And Moses said to the judges of Israel, "Each of you kill those of his men who have yoked themselves to Baal of Peor."*

> *And behold, one of the people of Israel came and brought a Midianite woman to his family, in the sight of Moses and in the sight of the whole congregation of the people of Israel, while they were weeping in the entrance of the tent of meeting. When Phinehas the son of Eleazar, son of Aaron the priest, saw it, he rose and left the congregation and took a spear in his hand and went after the man of Israel into the chamber and pierced both of them, the man of Israel and the woman through her belly. Thus the plague on the people of Israel was stopped. Nevertheless, those who died by the plague were twenty-four thousand. -Number 25:4-9 (ESV)*

Twenty-four thousand Israelites died because the people fell into the sex trap Balak and his nation presented to them. Thank God for Phinehas' action to stop the sin! But still, how devastating! Sexual sin always brings devastation.

- Families are destroyed when someone has an affair.
- Relationships with God are damaged when sexual sin takes root.
- Churches get destroyed when pastors and leaders sin sexually.
- Friendships get destroyed as marriages divorce, leaving people to choose a side.

The list goes on and on. The enemy entices you to sin, traps you, and then leaves you sprawled out on the mat.

If we want to be an unbreakable man, we need to defeat sexual sin and compromise in our lives.

I personally am so tired of seeing porn and sexual sin destroy men of God. I see it too often. Men have beautiful, amazing wives and fabulous children. But they fall into this trap and lose it all because they give in to the temptation.

I want to get really practical in this chapter and give you a path forward to win this fight. What practical steps can you take to help you stop losing the battle?

## 1. Acknowledge the struggle

You can't defeat something you refuse to admit is a struggle. It is hard to admit that you are struggling with sexual sin. It's so powerful because it carries shame, causing you to want to hide it. Acceptance and repentance are key! You won't gain victory until you are honest with yourself and God about your struggle with sexual sin. You must recognize that you cannot overcome it alone. You need God's help.

# UNBREAKABLE

1 John 1:9-10 tells us why this is so important.

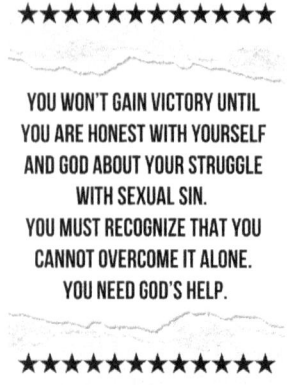

YOU WON'T GAIN VICTORY UNTIL YOU ARE HONEST WITH YOURSELF AND GOD ABOUT YOUR STRUGGLE WITH SEXUAL SIN. YOU MUST RECOGNIZE THAT YOU CANNOT OVERCOME IT ALONE. YOU NEED GOD'S HELP.

*If we say we have no sin, we deceive ourselves, and the truth is not in us. If we confess our sins, he is faithful and just to forgive us our sins and to cleanse us from all unrighteousness. -1 John 1:9-10 (ESV)*

You won't gain victory until you admit the sin and ask God to forgive you. The good news is He already knows the sin and is ready and waiting to forgive you.

## 2. Pray

Sometimes, we have to stop standing toe-to-toe and drop to our knees. Pray for God to forgive you. Ask for strength to fight. Ask God to deliver you from your sexual sin and to set you free from the grip of bondage it has on you.

If you don't know what to pray, try speaking in tongues.

> *Likewise the Spirit helps us in our weakness. For we do not know what to pray for as we ought, but the Spirit himself intercedes for us with groanings too deep for words. -Romans 8:26 (ESV)*

## 3. Guard your mind and heart

The best way to get the smut and prevision out of your mind that porn and sexual sin cause is to soak our minds in God's Word. Renew your mind with God's Word (Romans 12:2). Meditate on Scriptures that help you develop a pure mindset. Philippians tells us what to focus our minds on.

> *Finally, brothers and sisters, whatever is true, whatever is noble, whatever is right, whatever is pure, whatever is*

*lovely, whatever is admirable—if anything is excellent or praiseworthy—think about such things. -Philippians 4:8 (NIV)*

It is hard to sin sexually while reading the Word of God. It is hard to think of impure thoughts if you are thinking the thoughts of God found in His Word. When you are spending your time in the Word, you will gain victory.

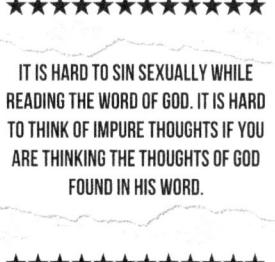

**4. Discover your weaknesses**

It is important for us to realize when we are most vulnerable to falling into sexual sin so we can take steps to avoid it.

- Does loneliness cause you to sin?

- Do you watch porn when you're bored and have nothing else to do?

- Does fighting with a family member or spouse lead you down this path?

- Does being isolated open you up to falling into this sin?

You have to discover your weaknesses to overcome them and grow in strength.

**5. Accountability**

Peer pressure is a great weapon when it comes to sexual temptation.

*Therefore confess your sins to each other and pray for each other so that you may be healed. The prayer of a righteous person is powerful and effective. -James 5:16 (NIV)*

We need men around us who have total access to us, can ask us any questions, and can hold us accountable for anything they see fit. Be an open book to them, allowing no question or topic to be off limits.

**6. Use technology to your advantage**

The bad thing about technology is the enemy has figured out how to use it for destructive attacks against a man's purity. The good thing about technology is that godly men have learned ways to safeguard against the enemies' attacks. Lots of tools are available to help God's man.

Use your TV V-chip to block out sexual content from your TV. Have someone else control the password so you don't succumb to temptation. The great thing about a V-Chip password is if you don't know it, you can't use it.

Use VidAngel, a service that removes sex and nudity from movies and TV shows.

Use the parental controls available on all internet browsers. There are programs like Net Nanny or Covenant Eyes that you can install on your computer. Not only do they keep you from being able to view porn on the internet, but they also send out email alerts to the men you choose to be accountable to, telling them what your web activity includes. When using these programs, don't forget to install them on your smartphones and tablets.

A side note: Often, when I tell men about these resources, the first thing they say is, *"I can't afford it."* Then, they proceed to ask why it can't be free.

First of all, you can't afford NOT to use these programs if you're struggling with porn. It may take sacrificing other things to pay for it, but victory is worth the cost.

Second, the reason they cost money is simple. Someone had to develop the program. Someone updates it. People maintain the program, and this costs money. They are not non-profits; they charge to cover their expenses. The worker is worthy of their hire.

I encourage you to take advantage of these technological advancements. It may cost you something, but freedom is worth the price.

**7. Rely on the Holy Spirit**

Jesus promised to send us a Helper. That Helper is the Holy Spirit.

The Holy Spirit cannot be joined with unholy spirits. His holiness cannot take the unholiness. Ask the Holy Spirit to lead and guide your life, and stay sensitive to His convicting power.

> ***But I say, walk by the Spirit, and you will not gratify the desires of the flesh. For the desires of the flesh are against the Spirit, and the desires of the Spirit are against the flesh, for these are opposed to each other, to keep you from doing the things you want to do. -Galatians 5:16-17 (ESV)***

Ask the Holy Spirit for help developing self-control and resisting temptation. Stay sensitive to His conviction; don't ignore it. We grow spiritually by allowing the Holy Spirit's power to work within us.

**8. Persevere in the journey**

There may be times that you stumble and fall back into sin. In a moment of weakness, you may fall. For every two steps forward, you may occasionally take a step backward. Don't let the setbacks cause you to return to your old way of life! Don't give up.

> *..for the righteous falls seven times and rises again..*
> *-Proverbs 24:16 (ESV)*

Get back up! Keep pursuing holiness even if you fall. God's grace is sufficient, and He will help you stand back up and get back into the fight.

**9. Focus on your identity in Christ**

Remember who you are in Christ.

> *Therefore, if anyone is in Christ, he is a new creation. The old has passed away; behold, the new has come.*
> *-2 Corinthians 5:17 (ESV)*

In Christ, you are forgiven, redeemed, and set free. Don't let shame or guilt destroy you. Instead, stand firm in the new identity God has given you. Remember, as God's son, you have all the power you need to defeat sexual sin.

> *I can do all things through him who strengthens me.*
> *-Philippians 4:13 (ESV)*

**10. Seek professional help if needed**

There is no shame in asking for help. If the struggle with sexual sin is more than you can handle, consider counseling. Seek the help of your pastor or Christian counselor to help you defeat the stronghold it has become in your life. They can offer practical tools and spiritual insights for healing and overcoming long-term struggles.

**11. When all else fails, RUN!**

In the Bible, we are constantly told to stand our ground, resist, and fight. However, when it comes to sexual sin, we are told to do the opposite.

> *Flee from sexual immorality. Every other sin a person commits is outside the body, but the sexually immoral person sins against his own body.*
> -1 Corinthians 6:18 (ESV)

We cannot yield to sensuality if we are running away from it.

Run for your life. Get out of there! If we try to reason with lust or entertain sexual thoughts, we will give in to them. We won't be able to fight it. This is why God forcefully orders us to run away from it.

Run with all your might.

Overcoming sexual sin is a lifelong battle for many, but with God's help, persistent prayer, and practical steps, victory is possible.

> ★★★★★★★★★★★★
> IF WE TRY TO REASON WITH LUST OR ENTERTAIN SEXUAL THOUGHTS, WE WILL GIVE IN TO THEM. WE WON'T BE ABLE TO FIGHT IT. THIS IS WHY GOD FORCEFULLY ORDERS US TO RUN AWAY FROM IT.
> ★★★★★★★★★★★★

Guys, we can't keep being defeated by the same trap that ensnared the Israelite men. It's time once and for all to defeat sexual sin and immorality in our lives! We must be vigilant and recognize the enemy's playbook. Let's stand firm, guard our hearts, and resist the enemy's temptations. It's the only way to live as unbreakable men of God, free from enemy snares.

It's time to take a stand and refuse to be defeated by the same old play. Are you ready to rise above and overcome? I believe you can do it!

## Group Study Questions

1. Have you ever played *Madden*? What team do you use?

2. When was the first time you remember seeing pornography? Where were you? How did it happen?

3. This chapter states, "*It is hard to sin sexually while reading the Word of God.*" Why is this true?

4. Which of the eleven points is the one that stood out to you the most?

5. Which one scared you the most?

6. Which one seems impossible to do? Why?

7. Are you willing to once and for all admit your struggle in this area and work to gain victory?

8. After reading this chapter, what is one thing you will put into practice or one thing you will change in your life?

9. How can we, as a group, help you do this?

# CHAPTER SIX
## THE SECRET TO SUCCESS

I am a Pennsylvania boy. I was born and raised here. It is the only state I have ever lived in. Being a South Central PA man, you'd think I'd be a die-hard Eagles fan. But I'm not. I have class (that line is going to get me some responses from all my friends who are Eagles fans). For instance, I wouldn't throw snowballs at Santa like the Eagles fans did…who wants coal for Christmas? Instead, I ride or die with the Denver Broncos and bleed orange and blue. When we win the Super Bowl, I won't be climbing any street polls!

I have been a passive fan of the other Philly area teams. I don't follow hockey, but I say I am a Flyers fan despite being unable to name one player. I am a lifelong Phillies fan who grew up on Mike Schmidt and Von Hayes, but today, I don't follow every inning of every game.

The same goes for the Sixers in basketball. I don't watch much basketball, mainly the playoffs, but I have a passing fandom for the Sixers.

When most people think of the Sixers, usually two things come to mind. First would be Allen Iverson ranting about practice. Second, you'd think of three words that the Sixers made famous.

*Trust the Process.*

This was the Sixers management's motto for many years while the team downright stunk. Any time fans complained, or people badmouthed the team, they'd say, *"Trust the process."* Whether or not the process worked is debatable, but they were committed to following the path and plan they had established.

The kings of Israel and Judah never reached their full potential as servants of God because they didn't trust the process. So many of them had the epitaph of being men who followed God. However, that epitaph would be tainted by one word.

**But.**

They followed God, BUT they didn't tear down the high places, aka, they didn't fully follow God. As a result, they never reached their full potential and often faced defeats and exile. Why?

Because they didn't trust the process. What do I mean?

God had very specific commands for how His people worshiped and served Him. He had a specific place to make offerings and sacrifices to Him, His Holy Temple in Jerusalem. He had precise ways to perform the sacrifices, ordained priests to make the offerings and order, and code for how to do it. He had a process. All Israel had to do to follow God and have His hand of protection was trust the process.

However, they didn't.

After King Solomon died, his son Rehoboam became king. Rehoboam was such a butt-head that ten of the twelve tribes rebelled against his kingdom and started their own kingdom, Israel. Rehoboam was left with just the tribe of Judah and Benjamin to rule over, and this was only because God had promised David his family would always have a kingdom and that the Messiah would come from this kingdom.

So, Israel's ten tribes left the kingdom and formed their own. They made a guy named Jeroboam their king. However, they didn't really choose him; God chose him.

> *The man Jeroboam was very able, and when Solomon saw that the young man was industrious he gave him charge over all the forced labor of the house of Joseph. And at that time, when Jeroboam went out of Jerusalem, the prophet Ahijah the Shilonite found him on the road. Now Ahijah had dressed himself in a new garment, and the two of them were alone in the open country.*
>
> *Then Ahijah laid hold of the new garment that was on him, and tore it into twelve pieces. And he said to Jeroboam, "Take for yourself ten pieces, for thus says the Lord, the God of Israel, 'Behold, I am about to tear the kingdom from the hand of Solomon and will give you ten tribes (but he shall have one tribe, for the sake of my servant David and for the sake of Jerusalem, the city that I have chosen out of all the tribes of Israel), because they have forsaken me and worshiped Ashtoreth the goddess of the Sidonians, Chemosh the god of Moab, and Milcom the god of the Ammonites, and they have not walked in my ways, doing what is right in my sight and keeping my statutes and my rules, as David his father did.*

> *Nevertheless, I will not take the whole kingdom out of his hand, but I will make him ruler all the days of his life, for the sake of David my servant whom I chose, who kept my commandments and my statutes. But I will take the kingdom out of his son's hand and will give it to you, ten tribes. Yet to his son I will give one tribe, that David my servant may always have a lamp before me in Jerusalem, the city where I have chosen to put my name.*
>
> *And I will take you, and you shall reign over all that your soul desires, and you shall be king over Israel. And if you will listen to all that I command you, and will walk in my ways, and do what is right in my eyes by keeping my statutes and my commandments, as David my servant did, I will be with you and will build you a sure house, as I built for David, and I will give Israel to you. And I will afflict the offspring of David because of this, but not forever.'"*
>
> *Solomon sought therefore to kill Jeroboam. But Jeroboam arose and fled into Egypt, to Shishak king of Egypt, and was in Egypt until the death of Solomon.*
> -1 Kings 11:28-40 (ESV)

God predicted everything that would happen and appointed Jeroboam to lead the ten tribes of Israel. All Jeroboam had to do was trust God, obey Him, and live for Him, and his kingdom and power would be secure. He would live as a successful king.

Easy-peasy, right?

Nope.

Jeroboam didn't trust God's process for His people. One reason he struggled with this was that right after God had appointed him king, he ended up on the run, in exile in Egypt, fearing for his life. Before God called him, he was an up-and-comer in Solomon's kingdom, praised and promoted by the King, on the fast track to success and a life of luxury and power. Then God called him, and he lost everything.

The splitting of the kingdom and still following God presented a problem for Jereboam. God commanded them to worship only at His Temple, in the heart of the kingdom of Judah, Jerusalem. Jeroboam wasn't too keen on all his people traveling to Jerusalem. He wasn't about to lose everything again!

> *Jeroboam said in his heart, "Now the kingdom will turn back to the house of David. If this people go up to offer sacrifices in the temple of the Lord at Jerusalem, then the heart of this people will turn again to their lord, to Rehoboam king of Judah, and they will kill me and return to Rehoboam king of Judah."*
>
> *So the king took counsel and made two calves of gold. And he said to the people, "You have gone up to Jerusalem long enough. Behold your gods, O Israel, who brought you up out of the land of Egypt." And he set one in Bethel, and the other he put in Dan.*
>
> *Then this thing became a sin, for the people went as far as Dan to be before one. He also made temples on high places and appointed priests from among all the people, who were not of the Levites.*
>
> *And Jeroboam appointed a feast on the fifteenth day of the eighth month like the feast that was in Judah, and he offered sacrifices on the altar. So he did in Bethel, sacrificing to the calves that he made. And he placed in Bethel the priests of the high places that he had made. He*

> went up to the altar that he had made in Bethel on the fifteenth day in the eighth month, in the month that he had devised from his own heart. And he instituted a feast for the people of Israel and went up to the altar to make offerings.-1 Kings 12:26-33 (ESV)

His trust in God was broken, and he feared failure as a king. He didn't believe God's promise of success and being blessed if he obeyed God. The last time he trusted God, he ended up with a death squad chasing him. So, he took matters into his own hands instead of following God's process. As a result, he lost God's blessing, and the entire nation suffered as they fell away from God and into idolatry.

Jeroboam, in a desire to keep his success, made his own system of worship, complete with golden calves, high places, fake priests, and imposter feasts. The stupid thing is, the only reason he got to be king in the first place was because Solomon worshipped idols…now he was doing the same thing! He opened up Israel to idolatry and walked away from following and serving God. This led them to follow deeper into sin.

Jeroboam had God offer the world to him, but he chose to do it his own way. How did his life end up? It ends with words of doom from the prophet God initially used to anoint him king.

Jeroboam's son Abidjan became deathly ill, so Jeroboam told his wife to disguise herself and go to the prophet Ahijah and ask him what would happen to the child. His wife left, but as she traveled to Abuja, God told the prophet she was not only coming, but she was trying to deceive him. Let's look at 1 Kings 14:6.

> When Ahijah heard the sound of her feet, as she came in at the door, he said, "Come in, wife of Jeroboam. Why do you pretend to be another? For I am charged with unbearable news for you. Go, tell Jeroboam, 'Thus says the Lord, the God of Israel: "Because I

*exalted you from among the people and made you leader over my people Israel and tore the kingdom away from the house of David and gave it to you, and yet you have not been like my servant David, who kept my commandments and followed me with all his heart, doing only that which was right in my eyes, but you have done evil above all who were before you and have gone and made for yourself other gods and metal images, provoking me to anger, and have cast me behind your back, therefore behold, I will bring harm upon the house of Jeroboam and will cut off from Jeroboam every male, both bond and free in Israel, and will burn up the house of Jeroboam, as a man burns up dung until it is all gone. Anyone belonging to Jeroboam who dies in the city the dogs shall eat, and anyone who dies in the open country the birds of the heavens shall eat, for the Lord has spoken it."'*

*Arise therefore, go to your house. When your feet enter the city, the child shall die. And all Israel shall mourn for him and bury him, for he only of Jeroboam shall come to the grave, because in him there is found something pleasing to the Lord, the God of Israel, in the house of Jeroboam. Moreover, the Lord will raise up for himself a king over Israel who shall cut off the house of Jeroboam today…And he will give Israel up because of the sins of Jeroboam, which he sinned and made Israel to sin."*

*When Jeroboam's wife arose and departed and came to Tirzah. And as she came to the threshold of the house, the child died. And all Israel buried him and mourned for him, according to the word of the Lord, which he spoke by his servant Ahijah the prophet. (1 Kings 14:6-14, 16-18, ESV)*

Jeroboam's rebellion against God and His ways cost him everything. His entire family and kingdom suffered. The sad part is that Jeroboam did it to keep his kingdom successful. But God had already promised him success if he did things God's way. His disappointment in how God did it and his fear of failing again caused him to not only not trust God but openly disobey God, and destruction ensued.

**FEAR OF FAILURE AND A HUNGER FOR SUCCESS AT ANY COST HAVE CRIPPLED TOO MANY MEN FOR TOO LONG.**

I believe this is a colossal trap so many men of God fall into. Fear of failure and a hunger for success at any cost have crippled too many men for too long.

We all hunger for success. We want to be the best at what we do. To achieve it, many men have put everything they have into their job and career. They don't sacrifice to idols to achieve it as Jeroboam did, but they do sacrifice for it.

- Marriages are sacrificed as they focus solely on careers and fame.

- Children are sacrificed as the job takes priority over them.

- Balance is sacrificed as they have tunnel vision of getting ahead, no matter the cost.

- A relationship with God is sacrificed as work and goals take precedence over prayer, Bible reading, and developing a relationship with God. They have no relationship with God because they make work the priority.

- Convictions and beliefs are sacrificed as people do things they know are wrong to get ahead or build the relationships they need to succeed.

- Integrity is sacrificed as they go against their morals and values or even break laws and rules to get ahead.

- Health is sacrificed as they work tirelessly at the expense of their mental, emotional, and physical health.

Chasing success in the wrong way destroys too many men, leaving them sprawled out on the mat, battered and defeated.

The sad part is that, like Jeroboam, God already guarantees success if we follow God and His process for our lives.

The ironic thing about Jeroboam is that his mentor, Solomon, eventually learned the lesson Jeroboam needed to know. In the book of Ecclesiastes, Solomon talks about his life. The dude had a good life! He built the original temple to worship God! He had fame, riches, women (too many women, as we already discussed!), success, and anything and everything he could have ever asked for. But he still felt like his life was empty and full of uselessness.

In the last verse of Ecclesiastes, he states his final conclusion on life: the one thing he decided matters more above and beyond everything else.

> *The end of the matter; all has been heard. Fear God and keep his commandments, for this is the whole duty of man. For God will bring every deed into judgment, with every secret thing, whether good or evil. -Ecclesiastes 12:13-14 (ESV)*

The Message version puts it more bluntly.

> *The last and final word is this:*
> *Fear God.*
> *Do what he tells you.*
> *And that's it. Eventually God will bring everything that we do out into the open and judge it according to its hidden intent, whether it's good or evil. -Ecclesiastes 12:13-14 (MSG)*

God promised Jeroboam: Follow me and do what I tell you, and you will succeed.

If he had only listened, the entire nation of Israel would have been so much better off!

What about you?

Why do you crave success so much?

Why do you fear failure?

Is something in your past causing you not to trust God?

Are you sacrificing everything on the altar of fame and success?

Has your life gotten out of balance because you are chasing after success in your own power instead of following God's path?

FOLLOW GOD AND DO WHAT HE TELLS YOU, AND YOU WILL SUCCEED.

Have you forgotten Jesus' command to seek His kingdom first and let Him bring everything else to you? (Matthew 6:33)

What is keeping you from trusting in God to do what He promised?

Men, I am tired of seeing my brothers in Christ defeated because they decide to pursue fame and success instead of following God and His process of living. I don't want to see men constantly defeated by pursuing the wrong kind of success. Today, decide to reverse course and start doing things God's way. This is the path an unbreakable man trods.

## Group Study Questions

1. Who are your favorite sports teams?
2. What effect did Jeroboam's being anointed and then having to flee for his life have on his ability to trust God's process?
3. Why do so many men struggle with wanting success?
4. How can chasing success cause us to end up defeated?
5. What is sacrificed in order to gain success?
6. What is keeping you from trusting God to do what He promised?
7. What steps can you take to stop this and become an unbreakable man?
8. After reading this chapter, what is one thing you will put into practice or one thing you will change in your life?
9. How can we, as a group, help you do this?

# CHAPTER SEVEN
## SHHH...IT'S A SECRET

It's the end of the day, and a man is closing the shop for the night. He is in a hurry to get to his softball league game that evening. He has just one job left to do. The boss trusted him to close out the cash register for the day, fill out the financial report, and deposit the money in the bank. As he counts the money and gets it ready, he slips a ten-dollar bill into his pocket. He has been doing it every few nights for the past few months and has accumulated a nice nest egg. He sees nothing wrong with it; it is only $10, and no one misses it. It is just his little secret.

Meanwhile, across the country, a man is on a business trip. He is a little bummed that he is going to miss playing in his softball league this week, but his job has to take precedence. At the meeting, he starts a conversation with another company employee named Tiffany. Tiffany is young and attractive, and he enjoys talking with her. She enjoyed it, too, because she asked him if he wanted to grab a bite to eat after the meeting. He unconsciously slips his hand with his wedding ring in his pocket as he thinks about the offer. He knows he shouldn't do it, but he is far from home, and no one will ever know. It will just be their secret.

Later that night, another guy is slipping into his local convenience store wearing a hat and sunglasses. He is sweaty and dirty after playing catcher in a league game. He self-consciously looks around as he walks to the cooler, reaches in, and grabs a six-pack of beer. He quickly pays and bolts for his car, hoping no one notices him buying alcohol. He feels a twinge of guilt that he is drinking again, but he quickly pushes it aside. After all, who would know?

Later that night, a man looks at his wife, who is sound asleep next to him, but he is restless and unable to doze off. He is still pumped up from hitting the game-winning home run in his softball game, catapulting his team into the playoffs. Her snoring isn't helping him sleep, either! He decides to get back up and work on his presentation for the big business meeting.

As he searches the net for a good graphic for his presentation, a pop-up flies on his screen. He sees an ad with a scantily clad woman in it. He knew he vowed the last time he looked that it would be his last time, but everything inside of him said, *"Look at it! It will relax you enough to sleep"*. Two clicks later, he's back in the stuff that secretly has bound him for years. But who is going to know?

A few days later, four guys sit in a local diner to have a bite together before heading to their church softball league. These four guys had committed to showing up early each week to spend time together before the game. It was how they did their weekly accountability group as they lived life together.

Bill mentions how great work has been going on lately as they sit and talk. He tells how his boss has him closing up every night and making the deposits. His friend says, *"See, that's the power of God in you that makes him able to trust you with his money."* He then jokingly asks, *"Aren't you ever tempted to help yourself to some of it?"*

Bill instantly panics. He knows he was lifting ten dollars frequently from his boss. He can't let this secret out! So, he quickly changes the subject by redirecting the conversation to Dave.

"Hey Dave, you been sleeping okay lately? I noticed Facebook had you logged in at one am the other night."

Dave begins to panic. How could he be so stupid as not to log out of Facebook? What if Bill figures out what he REALLY was doing when he was supposed to be working on his presentation after being unable to sleep? He begins to make some excuses, but Tom's annoying ringtone saves him.

"Man, Tom, shut that stupid song off. It is so annoying!" he jokes. He reaches over and grabs Tom's cell phone before he can grab it.

"Hey Tom, who is Tiffany? She is texting you to call her when you have some free time."

Tom's heart drops! How does he explain Tiffany? He told her not to call him on his phone, but now Dave saw her text!

Tom quickly makes up a lie and says, *"Oh Tiffany is an intern at the office. She probably can't find a file. I'll call her when we're done."*

Tom looks around at the guys. He thinks they bought his story, but to make sure, he quickly turns his attention to Jason. *"Jason, how long has it been now since you got saved? It's got to be, what, two years? I'll never forget how God saved you and delivered you from drinking. Are you ever tempted to drink again?"*

Jason calmly says, *"Nah, I am done with alcohol. But you know what? I had better start heading to the field. It takes forever to get the catchers' gear on, and it is soon time for the game."*

But inside, he is panicking. After the last game, he drank the last six-pack he bought at the convenience store. Why did Tom have to ask him about it?

The four men quickly finished their meeting, deciding they had better get to the field and get warmed up for the game. They are all anxious to get out of there before any more pointed questions are asked. After all, they need to make sure their secret sin stays just that —a secret. They get to the game and start throwing the ball around, all feeling guilty over their secret sin and wanting to confess it, but none willing to admit it.

While using stereotypical examples, this story is repeated repeatedly in our world today. Christian men across America have issues of sins inside of their lives that they work diligently to keep concealed. They fear anyone finding out because it would destroy their reputations as men of God. So they continue in their sin, secretly wishing they could be free of it, but not taking steps to overcome it. Instead, they let their unconfessed, hidden sins defeat them over and over again.

If we are going to write a book on becoming an unbreakable man, we have to examine the topic of unconfessed sin hidden in our lives.

If you're like me and have a sensitive conscience, the phrase *"unconfessed sin"* can send you into a tailspin. Suddenly, you're mentally scrolling through the past few days or weeks of your life, trying to remember if there were any times when you said, thought, or did something wrong and forgot to ask God to forgive you.

Let me put your mind at ease before you spiral down that rabbit hole. When we talk about unconfessed sin, it doesn't refer to sin we don't know about (ways we sin subconsciously). It isn't talking about occasional accidents, mistakes, or sins.

It doesn't refer to the day you weren't feeling well and snapped at your family or the time you accidentally swore when you dropped a brick on your foot. We're not talking about accidentally seeing an inappropriate scene in a movie while you were changing the channel, having a momentary inappropriate thought, or even forgetting to confess something to God in your time of prayer.

These things are not defiant actions. They are a part of being a human being. While we must keep short accounts with God and confess every sin the Holy Spirit brings to our minds, we can't beat ourselves up for every minor infraction. These things happen. You ask God to forgive you, and you move on.

Instead, when we say that unconfessed sin, we're talking about the sins that we struggle with over and over again and can't overcome or the sins that we choose to allow in our lives even though we know they are against God's Word.

We're basically saying, *"Come in and set up shop in my life because I have decided that this sin is more important to me than obeying God."*

Of course, most people don't say that part out loud, but their attitudes and choices show what's in their hearts.

One Biblical example of this is found in Joshua 7, in which we read the story of Achan. It's important to understand that Joshua 7 occurs just days after one of God's greatest miracles and Israel's most powerful victories in Jericho. Many of you will remember the story of the Israelites walking around the walls of Jericho every day for six days, and then, on the seventh day, God miraculously caused the walls of Jericho to crumble, giving Israel the distinct advantage to conquer their enemies.

God also gave them very clear instructions:

> ***Do not take any of the things set apart for destruction, or you yourselves will be completely destroyed, and you will bring trouble on the camp of Israel. Everything made from silver, gold, bronze, or iron is sacred to the Lord and must be brought into his treasury. -Joshua 6:18-19 (NLT)***

Simple enough..when you plunder the land, everything belongs to God. However, as we see in Joshua 7, Achan did not obey this command; instead, he took a robe from Babylon, 200 silver coins, and a bar of gold weighing more than a pound and hid it in his tent. (Joshua 7:21)

As far as Achan could see, no one was the wiser. Only God knew, and He was not pleased.

As we see in the beginning of Joshua 7, God could not continue blessing His people with victories until the sin was removed from their camp. Rather than having a mighty victory like they did in Jericho, when the Israelites attacked the much smaller town of Ai, they were defeated—big time.

Joshua and the Israelites were shocked. What happened?? What in the world was God doing? But when they prayed, they got a response they weren't expecting.

> ***But the Lord said to Joshua, "Get up! Why are you lying on your face like this? Israel has sinned and broken my covenant! They have stolen some of the things that I commanded must be set apart for me. And they have not only stolen them but have lied about it and hidden the things among their own belongings. That is why the Israelites are running from their enemies in defeat. For now Israel itself has been set apart for destruction. I will not remain with you any longer unless you destroy the***

*things among you that were set apart for destruction."*
*-Joshua 7:10-12 (NLT)*

Israel has a problem—someone in the camp sinned, but they don't know who or how. Notice that even though Israel has suffered a massive defeat and thirty-six men died, Achan still didn't confess his sin.

He didn't confess after God spoke to Joshua.

He didn't even confess when the Holy Spirit began putting a spotlight first on his tribe, then on his clan, then his extended family, then his immediate family, then finally on him. It wasn't until Joshua said, *"Dude, you're the guy, repent!"* that Achan said, *"I did it."* (Joshua 7:16-21) Let's be honest: confessing after you are caught isn't repentant; it's just getting caught.

Achan was very committed to not confessing his sin!

As we look at his story, we can see several elements that are common to the unconfessed sin that can cause us to become defeated, broken men.

### 1. Achan knew what God wanted and chose not to obey.

Achan didn't accidentally sin. It wasn't subconscious or a mistake. Achan knew what God said, but he chose to do the opposite.

He was disobedient and defiant.

These are two trademarks of unconfessed sins that cause strongholds in our lives. Whenever we know what the Bible says and choose to do the opposite, we are saying that our sin is more important to us than

★★★★★★★★★★★★
WHENEVER WE KNOW WHAT THE BIBLE SAYS AND CHOOSE TO DO THE OPPOSITE, WE ARE SAYING THAT OUR SIN IS MORE IMPORTANT TO US THAN OBEYING GOD.
★★★★★★★★★★★★

obeying God. Our choice to protect and defend our sin causes our repeated defeat.

## 2. Achan tried to hide his sin.

This is another tell-tale sign that unconfessed sin has a grip on your life—you have to hide it.

I've seen something throughout my life—unconfessed sin thrives on darkness and secrets. It's like fertilizer to a plant. The more you have to keep your sin quiet, the deeper the roots of the sin will go until it completely controls your life.

So if you have to hide it—you have a problem.

## 3. Even when Achan was called on the carpet, there was no sense of genuine repentance.

Even as we read Achan's confession after he was caught, we don't sense real remorse. He didn't ask his countrymen to forgive him for bringing them defeat, apologize to the families who lost their loved ones, or ask his own family for forgiveness for what he did to them. He doesn't appear repentant; he just got caught.

Again, this is a common attitude of someone with unconfessed sin. They aren't repentant. They don't find it necessary to confess their sin to God. They aren't sorry for how their sin hurts others. They may be sorry they got caught and have to suffer consequences, but if they had the choice to make again, they would have done the same thing. Here's one last element that is common in the unconfessed sin that defeats us.

## 4. You excuse your sin.

Granted, this is not found in the Biblical account of Achan, Still, it's so common we have to talk about it.

It's one of the biggest traps that allows people to condone their unconfessed sin rather than overcome it. We hear it all the time:

- *"But I can't help it, it's the way I was raised."*
- *"All the people in my ethnicity have this issue."*
- *"God understands, He sees what I've been through, and He knows I NEED this."*
- *"I have special circumstances. God's rules don't apply to me."*

And yet, the problem with excusing and defending our unconfessed sin is that, all the while, it is destroying us. It's damaging our relationship with God, hurting our conscience, setting up a stronghold in our lives, and saying, *"From here on, I'm in control. I'll be calling the shots."*

Here's the worst part—your unconfessed sin works for your enemy, and it is trying to destroy you.

While we may think we are fooling people, God, or even ourselves, the enemy of our souls knows that we have no intention of evicting this sin from our lives.

*So, how do we keep this from happening? How do we become unbreakable men who gain victory over our unconfessed sin if it is already there?*

## 1. We must be open and respond to the Holy Spirit's conviction.

One of the Holy Spirit's primary functions in the life of a believer is to convict us of the sin in our lives.

> **And when he comes, he will convict the world of its sin, and of God's righteousness, and of the coming judgment.**
> **-John 16:8 (NLT)**

The Holy Spirit convicts us as we hear God's Word, either as we read the Bible or listen to someone teach Biblical truth. Often, the Holy Spirit uses that truth to illuminate a sin in our lives and show us our need to repent and change.

Other times, the Holy Spirit will bring something to our memory when praying or in a time of worship. As we remember, we will feel a sense of conviction that shows us that we need to repent of a sin.

When this happens, it's like the Holy Spirit is standing in the house that is our lives, saying, *"This mess doesn't belong in God's holy house. We need to eliminate it and not allow it here again."*

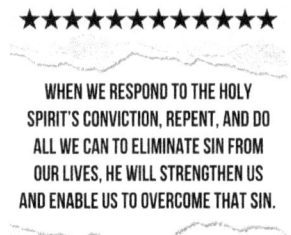

**WHEN WE RESPOND TO THE HOLY SPIRIT'S CONVICTION, REPENT, AND DO ALL WE CAN TO ELIMINATE SIN FROM OUR LIVES, HE WILL STRENGTHEN US AND ENABLE US TO OVERCOME THAT SIN.**

When we respond to the Holy Spirit's conviction, repent, and do all we can to eliminate sin from our lives, He will strengthen us and enable us to overcome that sin.

However, we all have to admit that there are times when we don't agree with the Holy Spirit and instead try to ignore Him. Perhaps we like the sin or believe we can't survive without it. Somehow, we've convinced ourselves that *"It's not that big of a deal"* or *"I need this in my life."* Maybe we've fallen for the lie that we cannot overcome it.

When this happens, sin can form a stronghold in our lives because we are protecting it.

But when we agree with the Holy Spirit's conviction, stop making excuses, and admit we have a problem, we are on the road to overcoming our sin and becoming an unbreakable man.

To achieve this, we need to follow step two.

**2. We need to see our sin as God sees it and hates it as much as He does.**

One of the biggest lies in today's world is that too many people believe the lie that *"Because God loves me, He thinks I'm adorable. When I sin, He thinks it's cute. He knows it's wrong, but because of His love, He understands. He knows what I'm going through or what I've been through, and He gets it."*

Feeding into this lie, churches today don't talk about *"sin."* Instead, they talk about people's *"messes," "issues," "mistakes,"* and *"problems."*

This makes it sound nicer, cuter, less dangerous, and less serious than it actually is. It's easier for people to hear. It's less offensive.

There's only one huge problem: in God's eyes, sin is offensive.

Because God is holy, He is pure and complete in character. He is totally without sin and right in everything He thinks and does. God's holiness means that He is separated from all evil. Sin literally offends Him.

If we are going to be honest with ourselves and other people, we need to take sin seriously, too. Because not only is sin a serious offense in God's eyes, but it also carries serious consequences.

The Bible says, ***"The wages of sin is death." -Romans 6:23 (NLT)***

This doesn't just mean the physical death that entered the world when Adam and Eve sinned, but the eternal death of life apart from God in Hell for all eternity.

The fact is that sin separates you from God.

Sin can keep you out of Heaven.

And sin will reap painful consequences here on earth.

*"But what about grace? What about mercy? What about forgiveness and God's love?"*

All of these things are absolutely true! They are all part of God's character and are available to everyone.

Without God's love, grace, and forgiveness, we would all be doomed to a life of destruction and eternity in Hell.

However, God's love, grace, and forgiveness are to remove our sins and give us a new life, not condone a sinful, unrepentant, rebellious life.

God sent His Son into the world to forgive sins and help us overcome them. While He is merciful and gracious in forgiving sin, that doesn't mean He condones it. Believing anything else is a big lie that only hurts the people who hear and believe it.

That's why you must stop excusing your sin, hiding it, playing around with it, and acting like it's no big deal.

You realize that sin is serious, and if it has taken up residence in your life, it must go.

### 3. You must confess your sin.

Once we hate our sin and are disgusted by it, once we realize that it hurts our relationship with God, others, and ourselves, we must confess our sins.

When *"…we confess our sins to him, he is faithful and just to forgive us our sins and to cleanse us from all wickedness."* -1 John 1:9 (NLT)

You must admit, "Yes, this is a big problem in my life. I recognize it. I agree with the Holy Spirit that this should not be a part of my life."

Then, you repent and ask God to forgive you.

In Psalm 51, King David sets an excellent example of how to repent when we have sinned against God.

It's interesting that even as a man who loved God, David fell into many of the same traps as Achan.

He knew God's Laws regarding adultery and murder, but still, he did it. Then, he tried to hide his sin, hoping no one would find out.

However, the big difference between Achan and David is that when David's sin was exposed, he immediately repented.

He recognized that his sin was a big deal.

He didn't make excuses, but he wholeheartedly and thoroughly repented.

Psalm 51 is the exact words that David prayed after he faced his sin. In this Psalm, we see some of the attitudes necessary to thoroughly repent of our sins and demolish any strongholds they may have in our lives.

First, David thoroughly confessed his sin.

>*Have mercy on me, O God, because of your unfailing love.*
>
>*Because of your great compassion, blot out the stain of my sins. Wash me clean from my guilt. Purify me from my sin.*
>
>*For I recognize my rebellion; it haunts me day and night.*
>
>*Against you, and you alone, have I sinned; I have done what is evil in your sight.*

> *You will be proved right in what you say, and your judgment against me is just.*
>
> *For I was born a sinner—yes, from the moment my mother conceived me.*
>
> *But you desire honesty from the womb, teaching me wisdom even there. -Psalm 51:1-6 (NLT)*

Next, David asked God to forgive him and cleanse him of all unrighteousness.

> *Purify me from my sins, and I will be clean; wash me, and I will be whiter than snow.*
>
> *Oh, give me back my joy again; you have broken me—now let me rejoice.*
>
> *Don't keep looking at my sins. Remove the stain of my guilt.*
>
> *Create in me a clean heart, O God. Renew a loyal spirit within me.*
>
> *Do not banish me from your presence, and don't take your Holy Spirit from me. -Psalm 51:7-11 (NLT)*

Finally, David shares his desire to stop sinning and live by God's ways.

> *Restore to me the joy of your salvation, and make me willing to obey you.*
>
> *Then I will teach your ways to rebels, and they will return to you.*
>
> *Forgive me for shedding blood, O God who saves; then I will joyfully sing of your forgiveness.*

> *Unseal my lips, O Lord, that my mouth may praise you. -Psalm 51:12-15 (NLT)*

This is such an essential part of repentance and overcoming our unconfessed sin: you do everything possible to get that sin out of your life and live differently.

You take a sledgehammer to it and destroy it. You demolish it. Whatever is necessary—whatever you must do—you do your part to get the sin and any stronghold it has formed out of your life.

This may involve:

- Confessing the sin to someone else.
- Finding an accountability partner.
- Finding a counselor for help or support.
- Making massive lifestyle changes.

It may take a combination of these things.

Still, true repentance means that whatever it takes to get this sin out of your life, you will do it.

Here's the amazing part: when you determine that you will do everything you can to remove sin from your life, the Holy Spirit that lives inside you partners with you to give you the strength to do everything you can't do on your own.

When your continued determination partners with the power of the Holy Spirit, together you can overcome any sin and tear down any stronghold from unconfessed sin in your life.

I love that David expresses this hope at the end of Psalm 51 when he says,

> *You do not desire a sacrifice, or I would offer one. You do not want a burnt offering.*
>
> *The sacrifice you desire is a broken spirit. You will not reject a broken and repentant heart, O God.* -Psalm 51:16-17 (NLT)

This is the hope for every person who is struggling with unconfessed sin in their lives—God wants to help you overcome the sin, tear down any strongholds that have formed, and walk in freedom and victory. Because He is gracious, merciful, and loving, He wants to forgive you and change your life. He doesn't want your sin to destroy you like Achan's sin destroyed him. He wants you to have a story like David's, filled with repentance, forgiveness, change, and victory.

> GOD WANTS TO HELP YOU OVERCOME THE SIN, TEAR DOWN ANY STRONGHOLDS THAT HAVE FORMED, AND WALK IN FREEDOM AND VICTORY.

Today, the choice lies with you.

Are you ready to stop excusing sin, protecting it, standing guard against the Holy Spirit, and saying, *"You can't touch this?"*

Will you recognize the damage sin is causing, repent, and partner with the Holy Spirit to do everything necessary to demolish it?

This is the only path to destroying unconfessed, hidden sin and becoming an unbreakable man. Repentance and demolition are your road to freedom and victory.

## Group Study Questions

1. What does it mean to have unconfessed, hidden sin? Why is it so hard to break free from unconfessed, hidden sin?

2. This chapter stated, *"Whenever we know what the Bible says and choose to do the opposite, we are saying that our sin is more important to us than obeying God."* How does this make you feel?

3. What role does repentance play in overcoming hidden sin? Why is it so difficult? Why is it so important?

4. Why do we believe God is ok with our sin? What does the Bible really say?

5. What was the difference between how Achan and David handled their hidden sin once it was exposed?

6. Will you recognize the damage sin is causing, repent, and partner with the Holy Spirit to do everything necessary to demolish it?

7. After reading this chapter, what is one thing you will put into practice or one thing you will change in your life?

8. How can we, as a group, help you do this?

# CHAPTER EIGHT
# THAT'S NOT HOW WE ALWAYS DID IT!

We discussed earlier how Rocky lost the fight to Clubber Lang In *Rocky III*.

*"Jamie, what is it with you and Rocky III?"*

What can I say? I LOVE this *Rocky* movie! Anyway, Rocky loses the fight, and he is defeated in more ways than one. He is not just physically beat. The fight also mentally destroyed him.

At this point, Apollo Creed enters the picture. He tells Rocky he lost the fight because he lost the *eye of the tiger*, and he was there to help him get it back.

Apollo takes Rocky to Los Angeles to the gym where Apollo Creed grew up fighting. He teaches Rocky a new way to train and a new style of fighting. They swim to build endurance, run to build speed, and dance to improve flexibility and footwork. They completely rework Rocky as a fighter.

Rocky and Paulie keep saying throughout these training segments, *"This isn't how we usually train"* or *"This isn't how we usually do things."* [1]

It was true. It was completely different. However, they had to train differently if they wanted different results from the fight. In the end, all the new techniques paid off, and Rocky reclaimed the title of Heavyweight Champion.

YOU HAVE TO TRAIN DIFFERENTLY IF YOU WANT DIFFERENT RESULTS FROM THE FIGHT.

One huge reason so many men stay broken and on the mat is that they get stuck in the mindset of doing things the way they have always done them. Often, we struggle because we have learned behavior in our past that we hold on to. Usually, we learn it from our parents. However, this can cause us to be defeated.

The fact is that we learn what we observe growing up. We develop what we will call generational patterns.

As children, we learn our family's beliefs, prejudices, behavioral patterns, and sins. Our parents teach us everything: how to talk, how to walk, how to eat, exercise, and sleep. We learn whether or not they see education as important and pick up their attitudes about work.

They teach us about relationships. They show us how people should interact with each other in and outside of a family. We observe how they talk to each other and about each other. We see what they do in public but also if they act the same or differently behind closed doors.

Our parents teach us about love, marriage, and family through observation. They show us how men and women respect or disrespect each other. Our families demonstrate to us whether or not children should be valued.

Families model how we should spend our time and our money.

Our families shape our views about government and religion.

As we grow in almost every area of life, we watch how the people we live with function, and we believe this is normal. In most cases, we consciously or subconsciously copy the ways of our ancestors.

Even those who determine that they do not want to live the way their parents did often find themselves falling into many of the same ways of thinking and reacting as their parents did unless they allow the Holy Spirit to work in their hearts, heal their minds and remove these thought patterns they learned from their parents.

This struggle of generational patterns can manifest in two different ways depending on whether you had a good or bad relationship with your parents.

Those who have had a problematic relationship with their parents or even an abusive relationship can fall into one of two traps. Either they can repeat their parent's destructive behaviors and choices and excuse it, saying, *"I can't help myself. This is the way I was raised,"* or they live as constant victims of their childhood, saying, *"I can't overcome. I'll always be defeated because of what my parents did."*

NO ONE IS DESTINED TO LIVE IN THE PAIN OF THEIR PAST. THROUGH THE POWER OF THE HOLY SPIRIT, YOU CAN BE HEALED OF THE PAIN OF YOUR PAST AND BECOME A COMPLETELY NEW PERSON MADE IN THE IMAGE OF CHRIST.

Neither of these paths is God's will for His children. No one is destined to live in the pain of their past. Through the power of the

Holy Spirit, you can be healed of the pain of your past and become a completely new person made in the image of Christ rather than the image of your parents.

No matter who your parents were or what they did—whether you were abused, whether your parent was an alcoholic, an inmate, or an angry person, even if your parent abandoned you—you are not destined to follow in their footsteps.

The Bible says that through Christ, you can become a new creation. Everything old can be healed and overcome, and you can become new.

> *Therefore, if anyone is in Christ, the new creation has come: The old has gone, the new is here! -2 Corinthians 5:17 (NIV)*

*But how is this possible—won't I always still be my parent's child?*

No, you can choose not to follow in their footsteps. While, yes, it is natural to repeat or reflect your parents, when you become a Christian, you become a child of God.

> *See what great love the Father has lavished on us, that we should be called children of God! And that is what we are! The reason the world does not know us is that it did not know him. -1 John 3:1 (NIV)*

As God's children, the Holy Spirit lives inside of us and is always at work in our hearts.

> *For all who are led by the Spirit of God are children of God.*
>
> *So you have not received a spirit that makes you fearful slaves. Instead, you received God's Spirit when he adopted you as his own children. Now we call him, "Abba, Father."*

> *For his Spirit joins with our spirit to affirm that we are God's children. And since we are his children, we are his heirs. In fact, together with Christ we are heirs of God's glory. But if we are to share his glory, we must also share his suffering. -Romans 8:14-17 (NLT)*

Look at what the Fire Bible says about verse 14:

*"The Holy Spirit lives within a true child of God in order to lead him or her to think speak and act according to the the principles, standards, and examples of God's Word."*[2]

Thus, because you are God's adopted child and because the Holy Spirit lives inside of you, no person is destined to repeat or reflect the sins or bad choices of their parent. When you become a Christian, you become a child of God, created to reflect His image. You can choose a different path because of the changing power of salvation and the Holy Spirit living in your life.

Now, to quote the late great Billy Mays, *But wait… there's more.* (Does anyone else remember those Oxyclean commercials?)

Not only are you not destined to repeat your parent's mistakes, but as a child of God, you are not doomed to living as a victim in the prison of what your parents did to you in the past.

As children of God, we are not called to be victims but victors. It is not God's will that you stay trapped in the prison of any physical, emotional, sexual, or mental abuse. You can be an overcomer through the work that Jesus did on the cross and the power of the Holy Spirit to heal you from your past experiences.

God has made a path forward for you that will heal the painful memories of your past.

You don't have to lie down and die, convinced that you will always be the victim of your parent's choice.

You can get up, put on your warrior's clothes, and do the work necessary to overcome every bad experience you had.

You can say, *"I'm not going to be a victim anymore…I will be free."*

As you make that choice, the Holy Spirit will partner with you to give you all the help, strength, courage, and wisdom you need to become a victorious child of God.

Here is the hope for everyone who has a challenging relationship with their parents:

You don't have to follow in your parent's footsteps.

You don't have to be a victim of your parent's failure.

As a child of God and a new creature in Christ, *"because of my parents"* doesn't have to be your prison.

You can overcome and become a new person who reflects the image of your Heavenly Father. How awesome is that!

Now to those on the other side of the coin: those with good relationships with their parents. Believe it or not, this can also become a trap that keeps us from being unbreakable.

Those with good relationships with their parents tend to get caught in the stronghold of wanting to do everything just like their parents did. They have so much respect, love, and loyalty for their parents that they cling to everything their parents did and want to repeat it. Sometimes, this is good if you follow a godly example. The problem comes when you make an idol out of the person you respect, and following in their footsteps becomes more important than following God's will for your life.

Here are some clues that this may be an issue:

- You care more about what your parent thinks than what God thinks of your choices. This can be a need for approval or a fear of disapproval.
- You refuse to see that your parent is a human being with faults and struggles of their own.
- You believe everything your parent says, does, and believes is Gospel truth.
- You struggle when the Holy Spirit leads you in a direction different from your parent's life.
- You argue with the Holy Spirit if He shows you that your parent's beliefs were not an accurate reflection of God's Word.

If you struggle with any or all of these things, you need to make some changes. Recently, my sister Adessa had to face this. I'll let her describe it in her own words.

*I (Adessa) learned the lesson of this second point through experience. While my book "Finding Healing" tells the story of how I learned the lessons of breaking patterns from a challenging relationship with a parent (my Dad), years later, the Holy Spirit started showing me some other destructive patterns that resulted from my relationship with my Mom.*

*Here's the thing: I had a good relationship with my Mom. Like all relationships, there were issues; she wasn't perfect, but it was that last line I had a hard time facing for a large part of my life.*

*When the Holy Spirit wanted to work on areas of my heart that resulted from fears or false doctrines I learned from my Mom, it freaked me out.*

*Because Mom and I were very close and because I knew her passion for Jesus and her love for her family, it was very difficult for me to face the truth that there were areas in her life where she was wrong. It was hard for me to face that much of what she taught me about a woman's role in God's kingdom came from the perspective of an abused woman. Even after God did miraculous work in our family and set us free from abuse, she was still working on overcoming the issues that came from years of being abused. Even though she didn't mean to, she passed on her fears and bad ideas she was taught to me.*

*This was really hard for me to face.*

*One of the reasons this way of thinking remained in my life for so long is that I guarded it. I protected it. I was so loyal to my Mom that I wouldn't allow the Holy Spirit or anyone else to point out ways she was wrong.*

*I couldn't begin demolishing strongholds in my life until I took my Mom off the pedestal I put her on growing up. I had to realize she was a fallible human being who had her own struggles, her own issues from her past and was on her own journey of experiencing healing. She was living through some challenging circumstances while tearing down her own strongholds.*

*As I've gone through this process, I've realized that I'm not the only one struggling. Many people have parents, grandparents, teachers, pastors, and even coaches who significantly impact their lives. They love them, respect them, and are appreciative of the positive influence they've had in their lives. They knew the heart of the person they loved and that they wanted to please God and do what was right. They were just human and hadn't overcome all of their issues.*

*Because of their loyalty, they are blind to the weaknesses of the person they love. They view them as infallible. Their words are always true. They try to live up to the standards they set.*

I appreciate Adessa letting me use her story.

What she described is much like the Israelites felt about Abraham, Moses, and David. To the Jews living in the New Testament, these men were heroes of the faith. They looked up to them, respected them, and wanted to be just like them.

Then Jesus—the literal Son of God—comes on the scene and starts teaching about fulfilling God's promises to Abraham, Moses, and David.

How do the people respond?

"But Moses said…"

"But Abraham taught…"

"David wrote…"

Here's the thing: these guys were great men. They were God's men fulfilling His purposes in their time.

But they were also human beings who had some big problems in their lives! They were far from perfect.

Moses killed a man. (Exodus 2:12) Even though he was God's man leading the people out of Egypt, he still had an anger management problem. We see it when he broke the original Ten Commandments (Exodus 32:19) and when he struck the rock when God told him to speak to it. God saw Moses' anger as such a problem that Moses could not enter the Promised Land because of his disobedience. (Numbers 20:1-13)

Abraham lied to get out of trouble (Genesis 12:10-20) and slept with his slave because he didn't believe God would fulfill His promise. (Genesis 16)

David committed adultery with Bathsheba, and his personal life and family were a mess. (2 Samuel 11-15)

Does this mean they weren't great men with close, personal relationships with God?

Absolutely not!

These men were the cream of the crop, the best of the best. Moses was so close to God that he had to wear a veil to hide God's glory, which shone off of his face after being with God. (Exodus 34:29-35) David was called *"a man after God's own heart"* (1 Samuel 13:14, Acts 13:22), and every future king of Israel and Judah was compared to him. Abraham was the father of many nations, and all who are justified by faith. (Romans 4, Galatians 3:29)

But they were also human beings. They were imperfect.

When we defend those we love and hold to the things they passed on to us rather than listen to the voice of the Holy Spirit, we follow the example of the Israelites who rejected Jesus to follow human heroes.

This just isn't right.

As God's children, we must follow God's ways and God's Word and fulfill God's purpose in our lives. When we can follow another's example as they are following God, that is great. However, whenever God leads us in a new direction or shows us the truth, we should never respond with, *"But that's not how my parents did it."*

We are called to follow God, not our parents.

Recently, when I started watching a new show called *"Buddy Valastro's Cake Dynasty,"* the Holy Spirit drove this point home to me.

I watched his first show, Cake Boss, many years ago on TLC. Back then, his children were babies, and the entire business occurred in a small business in Hoboken, NJ. I don't know if that show went off the air or I just got bored. Either way, it has been at least a decade since I watched it.

Now he's back with a new show, and everything is different. First, his kids (the babies and toddlers in the first ) are grown and working in the bakery. The business has grown, too. They now have bakeries and restaurants all over the country. Instead of working from a basement, the main headquarters is now a factory. It's a massive change.

Still, in almost every episode, Buddy talks about doing things the same way his father taught him to do them. He means he's still using the same recipes, still dedicated to quality, and working hard just like his Dad taught him. Yet, each time, I think, *"Let's be honest, there's nothing here like your dad did things."* All of the expansion brought massive changes.

The Holy Spirit has used this example to demonstrate the point of this chapter. Just like Buddy's business couldn't grow if he'd done everything exactly like his Dad did in the small family bakery, sometimes we need to let go of the *"way we've always done things"* or *"the way someone else did things"* so that we can grow and follow God's will for our lives.

The fact is that all growth necessitates change.

Change doesn't mean you disrespect or do not appreciate those who have come before.

Neither does admitting that those who came before us had struggles they didn't overcome.

It just means that, like Buddy, the Cake Boss, you are taking the foundation they gave you and building on it. You're taking their seed and allowing it to grow and expand.

I've learned that I can love and respect someone and still admit, "They were human. They had problems. Not everything I learned from them was good—some was really bad."

I'm learning that just because your parents were godly or did extraordinary things does not mean that you are destined to live exactly as they did or even live in their shadows. Our calling is greater than simply trying to fill someone else's shoes.

My identity is not just being my parents—it comes from being a child of God.

GOD'S PLAN FOR YOUR LIFE MAY ULTIMATELY DIFFER FROM HIS PLAN FOR YOUR PARENT'S LIFE.

The same is true for you: God's plan for your life may ultimately differ from His plan for your parent's life. He may call you to go further in life than your parents did, or He may call you to walk in a completely different direction altogether.

Whatever God's plan, we need to follow Him.

We need to build our own legacy.

So here's one last story: While I was working on this book, we were preparing for another year of Mantour Conferences. The theme was *"Unbreakable,"* and it had a boxing motif. I rewatched every Rocky and Creed movie to find quotes to put in that year's *Unbreakable Daily Bible Reading Plan.* I know, I sacrifice so much for you guys!

One day, while rewatching *Creed*, a scene jumped out.

Adonis Creed is preparing to fight when he receives a surprise gift from his mother, Mary Anne. This is a surprise because she was not thrilled that he was boxing and until then wasn't talking to him.

When the gift arrived, he opened it to find boxing shorts exactly like his father's, you know, the classic red, white, and blue shorts (which coincidentally Rocky wore when he beat Clubber Lang in *Rocky III* and Drago in *Rocky IV*). The only difference was that the name *"Creed"* was on the front, but Adonis' name, *"Johnson,"* was on the back.

The note that was attached said, *"Build your own legacy! -Ma."*[3]

The message was clear—fight and win the battle for yourself.

If you've ever seen Creed, you know this was a challenge for Adonis (Donnie). Born the illegitimate son of the great boxer Apollo Creed, young Donnie had a lot going on inside him.

He wanted to live up to his father's reputation as a boxer, yet he was angry at his father for dying and leaving him alone. Most of all, as he told Rocky near the end of the fight, he needed to prove to himself and the world that he wasn't a mistake. Emotionally, the dude was a mess.

That's why the message was so important. In those few words, Mary Anne said, *"It's time to stop living in the pain and anger from the past. It's also time to stop living up to your father's greatness. It's time to build your own legacy. Fight for yourself. Be who you were meant to be."*

This needs to be the attitude of every person who wants to become an unbreakable man.

We need to follow God and build our own legacy.

Forgive your parents for their failures.

Realize they were human beings with their own struggles and issues.

## UNBREAKABLE

Realize that you are a child of God and allow the Holy Spirit to help you heal, help you let go of the past, and learn to live as a child of God.

## Group Study Questions

1. What was your relationship with your parents like?
2. How can the way we were raised keep us from becoming unbreakable men?
3. Did the Holy Spirit shine His light on areas you have been following your parent's ways instead of God's ways?
4. What are the signs that we have made a godly parent or mentor an idol?
5. What does the example of the Israelites telling Jesus, *"That's not how our forefathers did it,"* teach us?
6. How can we admire someone's godly character traits without ignoring their flaws and failures?
7. What does it mean to *"Build your own legacy?"*
8. After reading this chapter, what is one thing you will put into practice or one thing you will change in your life?
9. How can we, as a group, help you do this?

# Chapter Nine
## BATTLE SCARS

I am a trilingual man. I am fluent in song lyrics, movie quotes, and sarcasm. I regularly interject any of these three into everyday conversation. Sometimes, out of nowhere, I will start quoting song lyrics in day-to-day chats to make the point I want to make.

I have always loved music. It has been an escape for me in hard times. My dad has often made the joke to me since I was sixteen years old: *"Do you know the car can still run without the radio being on?"* I guess he didn't like getting into the car and having music blasting at the top volume when he turned the key.

Music brings me joy and comfort, and often, God uses music to minister to me and even point out areas I need to work on.

I remember one day hearing a song that WRECKED me. Full disclosure: It wasn't a Christian song, but God still used it. The song spoke about how the person in the song was filled with fear, mistrust, anger, and pain because of their father. They couldn't have healthy relationships and were unable to trust anyone.

As I heard this song, something inside of me broke. I was filled with anger and rage, but more importantly, my heart was broken and filled with tears and pain.

I couldn't run from it. I couldn't get away. I tried to shut it out and stop it, but a dam broke inside of me, and years of hurt, pain, and repressed memories flooded me.

I remembered things I hadn't thought thought about in years. I had flashbacks to things I had completely blocked out of my head and memory. I relived moments of abuse, pain, and trauma that I had buried inside for decades. I could feel the fist hitting me. I could hear the cruel words spewed out at me.

I had buried it and repressed it. I buried so much so deeply that I had years of my life I couldn't remember. But suddenly, it all started to unravel.

Thankfully, I had a mom I could trust to talk about these issues. More importantly, I had the Holy Spirit who could help me face the pain and trauma and work through it.

The funny thing is, I didn't realize how much of this trauma I had buried and repressed still manifested in my life and left me sprawled out on the mat, beaten and broken.

While there have been times when I have had to deal with hidden sins in my life (this is a part of every Christian's life) and generational patterns I learned, most of the struggles and sins in my life have come from these unresolved issues from my past.

I don't believe I am alone. I think trauma from our past is defeating and breaking so many men of God.

This can include things that you have done or were done to you, as well as your experiences and the effects those experiences have had on your life.

Our experiences affect us for better or for worse. They influence how we view God, ourselves, and those around us. They alter our belief systems and influence our thinking.

Apart from the work of the Holy Spirit in our lives, we are the product of our experiences. We carry those experiences, the things that happened to us, and the words spoken to and about us in our hearts and minds as if we were carrying a backpack.

Some of our life experiences were very good. However, we can all agree that we've all experienced things in our lives that were traumatic and that caused us pain.

Often, because we don't want to deal with the pain or we can't deal with the pain because of immaturity or circumstances at the time, we push the pain to the back of our minds and forget about it, hoping that it will go away.

We bury it or cover it up. Another term is that we *"repress it."* The problem is that unaddressed, unhealed pain in our hearts doesn't go away. It just hides and creates a stronghold in our lives. Here's how my friend, Laverne Weber, describes it in her book, *"Victory's Journey"*:

*"Everybody carries some junk in their backpack that they really don't need. Whether big or small, that junk weighs us down and keeps us from being all that God wants us to be.*

*In dealing with the healing of past pain, we need to identify past pain.*

*The past is anything before today. It can be from your childhood or from later in your life.*

*Pain is something that has caused you to suffer. That suffering cripples you and prevents you from being all that God intended you to be....*

*Different people react differently to pain. That can be a way of coping. God gives us the ability to shut down areas of emotion and memory when we are not able to deal with the distress. There may be whole blocks of time that seem to be missing in a person's life. The person knows something is wrong but may not be sure what it is. Other people know what happened but have shut down any emotional response. After a while, they find they have difficulty even feeling good feelings. Some people wear "masks". At first, this helps to cope with the hurt, but in time, these masks become walls to hide behind.*

*Often, hurting people just don't know how to come out into freedom.*

*Others ignore the pains of the past...*

*Pain that is not dealt with will find another way out, and it will often hurt someone else. It is so much better to go back prayerfully and be healed.*

*One of the first steps in the healing process is to identify the pain."*[1]

She goes on to describe the five types of pain:

*1. Physical - severe illness or injury to yourself or a loved one*

*2. Spiritual*

*3. Emotional – hurtful relationships and rejection*

*4. Negligence – abandonment, lack of proper care and provision*

*5. Sexual (may be subtle or suggestive) – any violation of privacy in the sexual area*[2]

When left unaddressed, all of these types of pain can create powerful and painful strongholds in life. This means that our past experiences influence how we think, react, feel, and make decisions.

So, how do we overcome the pain and trauma from our past experiences so that we can think, react, and make choices through God's eyes rather than the eyes of our pain?

Once again, we must allow the Holy Spirit to show us His truth.

For me, it usually starts with a *"trigger."* I'll see a television show or a movie, or I'll hear a song, and it will hit my heart in an unusually painful manner.

Even as I use the word *"triggered,"* I cringe because it's been misused today. Too many people believe that if something *"triggers"* them or causes emotional pain, they need to do all they can to avoid the thing causing the pain.

However, this is the wrong attitude. Instead, we should see the *"trigger"* as a blessing because it shows that we have an issue in our hearts or minds that needs to be healed. Once we realize the problem is there, we can get to the root of the problem, face the pain, and allow the Holy Spirit to heal us.

★★★★★★★★★★★★

WE WEREN'T MEANT TO LIVE TRAPPED IN THE PAIN OF OUR PAST. GOD NEVER INTENDED FOR US TO BE PRISONERS, TRAPPED BY OUR MEMORIES AND HIDING FROM OUR "TRIGGERS." INSTEAD, GOD'S WILL IS FOR US TO OVERCOME OUR PAST BY EXPERIENCING COMPLETE HEALING AND THEN USE OUR VICTORY TO HELP OTHERS GOING THROUGH THE SAME STRUGGLE.

★★★★★★★★★★★★

Here's the truth: we weren't meant to live trapped in the pain of our past. God never intended for us to be prisoners, trapped by our memories and hiding from our *"triggers."* Instead, God's will is for us to overcome our past by experiencing complete healing and then use our victory to help others going through the same struggle. (Romans 8:37-39) This can only happen when we face pain in our lives.

How do we do this?

As I said, the first step is to allow the Holy Spirit to show you the source of your pain when something triggers it.

In addition to convicting us of sin, the Holy Spirit can also lead us into truth.

> **When the Spirit of truth comes, he will guide you into all truth. -John 16:13 (NLT)**

This includes helping us remember the things from our past that are causing pain in our hearts. That's what happened with the song I mentioned earlier. I was completely surprised at the emotion it stirred up. So I prayed and asked, *"What is going on? Why is this happening?"*

Before long, the Holy Spirit began helping me remember moments from my childhood that I hadn't thought about in fifteen-plus years. Sometimes, I'd remember things as I prayed; other times, the memories would resurface in dreams. Sometimes, while going about my day, I would remember something. I often asked my sister and mom, *"Did this really happen? Am I remembering this correctly?"* only to hear, *"Yeah, it happened. And this happened, too."*

No matter how it happened, each time I asked the Holy Spirit to help me, He brought the correct memory to the surface in the right way and at the right time. Then, He was there to comfort me through the next step of feeling the pain of the memory.

Because here's the thing about repressed memories—we bury them for a reason. They hurt!!

The hard truth about dealing with our repressed memories is that you will not only remember what happened, but you will most likely feel the pain again.

For instance, there was one particular area from my childhood that has caused me pain for years. Even though it may not seem like a big deal to others, it caused so much trauma in my life that I had nightmares about it for decades. Then, the Holy Spirit led me to a time of facing the truth about my past that I would never face before.

It HURT remembering it. However, the momentary tears and heartache of actually facing the pain led to my freedom. Having faced the pain, it didn't have control over me. Facing the pain and dealing with it set me free. Now, I can remember my past, but the pain is gone!

The pain of the event left my heart like puss leaves a pimple. (Gross, I know, but accurate.) Even more importantly, as time has gone on and the wound has healed, the pain no longer keeps me in its prison. Even if the anxiety tied to this event tries to resurface, I can now logically tell myself, *"It's over. It wasn't right when it happened, but it won't happen again,"* and move on.

That is what made all the temporary and momentary pain of remembering worth it—the freedom I live in now.

Of course, the process didn't end with remembering. There was still the recovery process.

We must allow ourselves the time that we need to heal—not a time to wallow, but a time to rest, sometimes cry, heal, spend time with Jesus, and soak in God's Word.

Yes, I understand that it's often impossible for us to walk away from our daily responsibilities. However, when you are in a time of healing from past pain and tearing down strongholds, you need to be intentional about making life slow down a little. Yes, you still have to do what's necessary, but during this time, you will probably have to cut back on the *"unnecessary"* to make time to rest. (After all, inner healing and tearing down strongholds is hard work!)

During this time, you must prioritize spending time with Jesus—not interceding for the whole world but talking to Him about what's happening inside you. Share your heart openly and honestly. Don't be surprised if He speaks words of Scripture or comforts you back.

Remember: God wants you to heal and be free. He's pulling for you and will do all He can to help as you spend time with Him.

It's also essential that as you're healing, you prioritize time in God's Word.

Why?

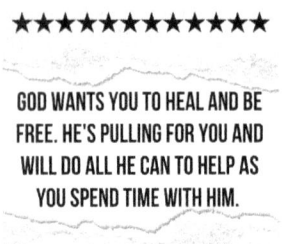

GOD WANTS YOU TO HEAL AND BE FREE. HE'S PULLING FOR YOU AND WILL DO ALL HE CAN TO HELP AS YOU SPEND TIME WITH HIM.

God's Word will help you see how to move forward. Your life will be very different as you live without the pain in your heart. God's Word can show you how to rebuild.

The truth is that trauma is a lot like a hurricane or a tornado. The storm blows in, and it's horrific to live through, but then it goes away. The problem is that even though the storm has passed, it often leaves incredible devastation behind.

When we ignore the pain in our hearts, we are like people who choose to ignore the damage the storm did to their homes. It's like living with broken windows or a house with no roof. Rather than dealing with the water damage, they ignore it, allowing it to breed mold and pollute the air they breathe daily.

Most storm victims choose the better path: after the storm has passed, you clean up the mess. You fix what is broken—tear off the old shingles and remove the water-damaged drywall. Then, you replace what has been damaged with new materials and rebuild.

That's what we need to do with the trauma in our lives.

Whether a storm went through your life yesterday or decades ago, the hope is that you don't need to continue living with the damage.

Through the power of the Holy Spirit, you can overcome the pain in your heart, experience healing, and rebuild your heart and mind. You don't need to continue carrying the hurt in your past around in your mental book bag any longer.

You can experience healing.

You can have a brand new start.

Next to salvation, the Bible, and the Holy Spirit, emotional and mental healing is one of God's greatest gifts to His children.

It gives us freedom from our past and new hope for the future. It allows us to find deliverance from bondages and lies that are holding us captive and keeping us from experiencing the abundant life that God has for us.

> ★★★★★★★★★★★★
> NEXT TO SALVATION, THE BIBLE, AND THE HOLY SPIRIT, EMOTIONAL AND MENTAL HEALING IS ONE OF GOD'S GREATEST GIFTS TO HIS CHILDREN.
> ★★★★★★★★★★★★

It is one of the central reasons that Jesus came to earth and died on the cross for our sins.

> *Surely, He took up our pain and bore our suffering, yet we considered him punished by God, stricken by him, and afflicted.*
>
> *But he was pierced for our transgressions, he was crushed for our iniquities; the punishment that brought us peace was on him, and by his wounds we are healed.*
> *-Isaiah 53:4-5 (NIV)*

Jesus came so that we could experience healing and freedom from the pain of our past.

Today, I don't know what wounds you are facing.

I don't know the issues in your life that the Holy Spirit may ask you to address and overcome.

I know this: You can give yourself no greater gift than responding to God's offer of healing.

Don't let the fear of painful memories or rocking the boat from the truth that God wants to uncover keep you in bondage.

Will there be pain?

Yes. For a little while.

Could learning the truth and tearing down strongholds cause problems?

Yes. However, it won't really cause the problems. It will just uncover existing problems and reveal ways to find solutions.

Ultimately, any pain or difficulty you go through will be worth the effort to gain freedom.

God's healing allows temporary pain to remove the pain that is crippling our lives and keeping us from spiritual and emotional health.

When we allow the Holy Spirit to do His work, we will find that the Great Physician can carry us through the pain, through our recovery, and bring us to a place of unimaginable healing and freedom. We can stop letting our past trauma defeat us and start living the life of an unbreakable man!

## *Group Study Questions*

1. As you read through this chapter, did the Holy Spirit bring any areas of trauma or repressed pain to your mind?

2. Do you know of anything that triggers you?

3. How can you use these *"triggers"* as a catalyst for healing and deliverance?

4. How does the the Holy Spirit's role to lead us into truth help us overcome the trauma in our lives?

5. What steps will you take to overcome the repressed pain in your heart?

6. After reading this chapter, what is one thing you will put into practice or one thing you will change in your life?

7. How can we, as a group, help you do this?

# CHAPTER TEN
# MONEY MAKES THE WORLD GO AROUND

*Money? Why are we talking about money in a book about being unbreakable? Unless you're talking about breaking a piggy bank or being broke, how does it fit this book? Is this really necessary?"*

Of course it is! I truly believe that a man who wants to be unbreakable must change his financial life and money management. So, that is what we are going to discuss in this chapter.

The first area I want us to examine is the need for an unbreakable man to show our thanks to God for allowing us to spend His money. Does that sound like an odd way to word that sentence? After all, we work hard and earn our money.

But the reality is that God allows us to earn the money. He supplies the job, and He expects us to be good stewards of the money. Part of being a good steward is doing something called tithing.

Tithing is when we give God 10% of the money He gives us back to Him via our local church. It is God's will for all men to tithe 10% of their paychecks, not the leftover part. We give God 10% before the government helps themselves to some.

That sounds like a drag, right? After all, times are tough, people are struggling, and we need every dollar we have. Why do we have to give 10% back to God?

I recently saw a man I know on Facebook with this exact question. This man is constantly living a defeated life, stretched out on the mat, unable to get up. He has a lot of issues in his life that he isn't facing and overcoming. Now, he is asking why he needs to tithe when money is tight. All I could think was how this decision not to tithe would cause him more defeat and heartbreak!

Why? Because the Bible is very clear. If you want the blessing of God on your life and finances, you have to tithe. If you don't tithe to Him, He won't bless you.

No man can expect to grow and prosper in God's kingdom without tithing. Why? Because the Bible says that a man who doesn't tithe is a man who is stealing from God. Malachi 3:8-10 says:

> *"Will a mere mortal rob God? Yet you rob me.*
> 
> *"But you ask, 'How are we robbing you?'*
> 
> *"In tithes and offerings. You are under a curse—your whole nation—because you are robbing me. Bring the whole tithe into the storehouse, that there may be food in my house. Test me in this," says the Lord Almighty, "and see if I will not throw open the floodgates of heaven and pour*

*out so much blessing that there will not be room enough to store it." (NIV)*

Do we think God will bless and grow us spiritually if we steal from Him? Yet it clearly says you steal from God when you don't tithe. God even says He can't bless you and offers a challenge to try tithing and see if He doesn't prosper you. So men need to be faithful and give God 10% of our money, and we need to do it happily, thanking Him that He provided us with the other 90%. Seriously, a man of God cannot afford not to tithe.

Tithing isn't the only area of finances we need to look at if we live as unbreakable men. God not only wants men to give Him back 10%, but He also wants us to be good stewards over the other 90% He allows us to keep. God doesn't ask it. He demands it!

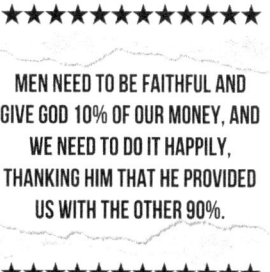

MEN NEED TO BE FAITHFUL AND GIVE GOD 10% OF OUR MONEY, AND WE NEED TO DO IT HAPPILY, THANKING HIM THAT HE PROVIDED US WITH THE OTHER 90%.

Living on a budget is the best way to ensure we are good stewards of God's money. A budget keeps us focused on how we spend the money and helps us avoid debt.

Regardless of age or economic level, every man must live on a budget. A budget is a plan. It tells you how much money you have and where it must go. It provides boundaries for how much can be spent in an area. It also provides freedom because you know that when you need something, the money is there.

Living without a budget is like trying to build a house without blueprints. You can't keep adding stairways, pipes, or wires without knowing how much of each is needed and where it is going. In both cases, you'll have the same result—A BIG MESS. Living on a budget avoids the big mess. It gives you a plan to follow to avoid financial destruction. It is an absolute necessity.

A lot of guys freak at the word "*budget*." They can't imagine living with a structured financial system that doesn't allow you to buy what you want when you want it and let it all ride on the credit card. The structure and confines of a budget seem so restricting. However, it is the exact opposite.

Rather than being restrictive and oppressive, a budget is freeing. Knowing there is enough money to pay all the bills when they are due releases enormous money stress. A budget's boundaries let you know how much you can spend. If you stay within the restraints of the budget, you can live without the pressure of consumer debt. It is great!

Whether you are a teenager with an allowance or a job, a college student learning to live within your means while balancing tuition, rent, car payments, and living expenses, a father managing a family budget, or even a grandpa enjoying your retirement, you need to budget your money. Living on a budget can avoid many money pitfalls.

I've seen too many men's lives damaged or destroyed because they didn't live on a budget or maintain a financially sound lifestyle. Instead, they let their appetites for things knock them down.

What do I mean by appetites?

You can't discuss money without discussing appetites. Why?

Too often, we get into financial trouble because we use money to meet our inner needs or to make us feel like a big man. Sometimes, we use money to buy friends or gain the esteem of others. Money can be a superficial balm to soothe our issues and insecurities. But these practices will leave us in debt and still having the issues. Money doesn't fix any problems. Only God can fill our needs and appetites.

We have to learn to curb our appetites for things. One of the biggest areas this involves is moving past our need for instant gratification and beginning to manage and save our money wisely. We do this by learning to curb our appetites. Why?

Ultimately, it's the appetites in our souls that cause us to spend money rather than save it. Until we deal with the deficiencies causing our appetites, we'll never be able to overcome the problem of deficient funds in our savings accounts and living on a budget.

Let's start by defining what I mean by "*appetite.*"

An appetite is a craving inside the soul that has never been satisfied. It is striving after or towards something. It is something yearned for or longed for that is never filled or satisfied. We use a variety of things and ways to fill this craving.

Appetites operate from our soul, the seat of our emotions, then through the heart and mind. They consume as much of the mind as they can. We want and want, but nothing satisfies. So we buy and buy and end up in debt.

Solomon describes it this way in Ecclesiastes 6:7: ***"All the toil of man is for his mouth, yet his appetite is not satisfied."*** **(ESV)**

What causes us to have appetites?

Some people have appetites based on deep, unmet soul needs. They think satisfying their appetites through instant gratification will fulfill their emotional needs.

Some appetites come from trying to prove to someone else that we are better than them. This can consume our lives, causing the tendency to become workaholics.

Some allow appetites to take the place of God. Things are used to fill the void only God can fill.

Some have appetites as adults because they grew up poor and resolved never to be poor again. So they work more and more to buy more and more. They live extravagantly and are usually in debt. We have all kinds of unfulfilled needs in our souls because we live in an imperfect world and were raised by imperfect people. This is all a part of life.

I know that my life was a mixture of these reasons. As a child, I was always told we couldn't afford to live like everyone else, so I decided that when I was older and had my own money, I would never do without the things everyone else had. I also spent money to make myself feel like a big man, easing the feelings of inadequacy I faced because of my physical disabilities. I used money to buy things to ease the pain of years of abuse. All this to say, I used money to meet my emotional needs deep inside, and, as a result, I didn't handle money maturely or responsibly. Instead, I was bound and chained to my childish ways. I had to face my childish ways and let the Holy Spirit teach me how to handle money properly. He did this by making me begin by facing my appetites.

Appetites, no matter their origin in our soul, want us to entertain the flesh by keeping busy, keeping occupied with the things in the world, doing all kinds of activities, working, overeating, shopping, living for sports, and worshipping the body. They make the flesh desire happiness, and we will do whatever it takes to make our flesh happy. All these activities and things eat up our money in today's world. So, we spend and live beyond our budgets to live in debt.

Can you see why we need to address the issue of our appetites to be able to budget money and live financially responsible lives?

Realistically, the reason Americans are struggling so severely financially isn't a *"financial"* problem. Even in these tough financial times, our incomes are still among the highest in the world. Yes, inflation is bad, and everything costs more. However, the reason that many Americans struggle is that our lifestyle expectations and our emotional appetites are controlling our lives rather than our common sense.

We spend money we don't have to satisfy our emotional needs when we should allow God to heal and satisfy our emotional needs and use common sense to manage our money. One key to getting your financial house in order is realizing how your emotional needs and appetites affect your spending habits.

How do we do this?

First, we need to start with prayer. We need to ask the Holy Spirit to show us our appetites and what emotional needs those appetites are trying to fill. Sometimes, we have to look at the lives of our parents, grandparents, and great-grandparents and see what they lived for and what made them happy.

What made them feel good and successful? How did they spend their money?

What did they do with their time? How did they spend their money?

**WE SPEND MONEY WE DON'T HAVE TO SATISFY OUR EMOTIONAL NEEDS WHEN WE SHOULD BE ALLOWING GOD TO HEAL AND SATISFY OUR EMOTIONAL NEEDS AND USING COMMON SENSE TO MANAGE OUR MONEY.**

We grew up watching them and imitating their behavior and practices. God has to cleanse us from their sinful and wrong uses of money and develop His ways in us. Learning from the past is very valuable. You can see what needs to change inside of you and the direction God needs to take you.

Another question is, *"How did my parent's or grandparents' actions affect my life?"*

Did your parents meet your emotional needs or leave an empty void inside?

Did you have physical restraints that didn't allow you to be like all the other kids?

Were you poor growing up, and did others make fun of you? Appetites can drive us to buy things we think we missed growing up. We convince ourselves we need them.

After you've looked at your past, you need to look at your present. Ask yourself some questions like:

What are my appetites? What do I live for? What consumes my time?

What do I have desires for in life? Are they for God? This world? Money? Clothes? Sports? TV? Cars? What? What do I hunger and thirst for deep inside my soul?

What do I set my eyes on?

What does my heart lust after?

What do I spend my time on?

Once we know the answers to these questions, we will start to recognize our appetites---the emotional issues screaming, *"Feed me, or I'll die!"*

The next question is, *"How do we change? How do we get rid of our appetites?"*

First, you need to recognize your specific appetites and what you do to fill them.

Do you shop when you're sad?

Do you spend money when you're bored?

Do you buy new expensive "*toys*" you can't afford because you're lonely?

Are you trying to buy your wife's or your children's love? The first step to overcoming is recognizing how your appetites affect your behavior.

Next, you need to confess your appetites to God. Proverbs 28:13 says, *"People who conceal their sins will not prosper, but if they confess and turn from them, they will receive mercy." (NLT)*

Ask God to forgive you. Ask Him to forgive you for putting your cravings first in your life before Him.

Change your mind and lifestyle by reading the Bible and obeying what it says. Ask God to lead you in your new financial journey to freedom. I know this is a prayer God will answer because it aligns with His will!

We can't keep letting our love for money, poor stewardship, and appetites keep knocking us down and breaking us. God longs for His sons to be faithful with their finances.

He wants men who appreciate the many blessings He gives them and shows this appreciation by tithing 10% and being good stewards of the other 90%.

He desires His sons to use money to meet their physical needs instead of their emotional needs and longings. God calls us to be unbreakable men who use money properly, not letting our appetites and insecurities financially drain us.

## Group Study Questions

1. Why is financial responsibility an important part of being an unbreakable man?

2. Do you tithe? If so why? If not, why not?

3. What does it mean to be a good steward of the remaining 90%

4. What are some reasons for living on a budget? Do you live on a budget?

5. How do our appetites affect our finances?

6. What is an appetite you have to guard against in order to handle money like a godly man?

7. After reading this chapter, what is one thing you will put into practice or one thing you will change in your life?

8. How can we, as a group, help you do this?

# CHAPTER ELEVEN
## ONE MORE ROUND

*"I didn't hear no bell yet, one more round."*[1]

This a phrase you'll hear around our house a lot.

Because my sister speaks fluent *Rocky* (in all fairness, I'm also fluent in *Gilmore Girl*), she knows exactly what it means.

It comes from *Rocky V*—the one with Tommy Gunn. (Did you really think I could write the final chapter about being *unbreakable* without one last Rocky reference?)

*Rocky V* is the least successful of the *Rocky* movies; honestly, it wasn't the greatest movie. But it does have some good moments. In the movie, an older Rocky can no longer fight because of an injury to his brain from his fight with Drago. To make things worse, Rocky has all of his money embezzled, leaving him broke. He has to sell everything and move back to his old neighborhood.

Rocky reopens Mighty Mick's Gym and starts training fighters when he meets Tommy Gunn, a hungry fighter who is not a good man. He was the epitome of Rocky's phrase *"a bum."* But Rocky can't see this even though everyone else can see the truth. Eventually, Tommy turns on Rocky.

The movie's last scenes are when things come to a head with Rocky and Tommy as they end up having an all-out street brawl. At one point, Tommy Gun knocks Rocky to the ground, and he thinks the fight is over. But Rocky, drawing strength from the memories of everything Mick had taught him over the years, which he in turn tried to teach Tommy, gets back up and says, "*I didn't hear no bell yet, one more round."*[1] Then he gets back up, fights again, and wins.

I use the phrase, *"I didn't hear no bell yet, one more round"* all the time. At first, when I started quoting this line, my sister hated it. She'd be annoyed when we were in the middle of a big project or a series of events, when we'd be tired and want to rest or even give up, and I'd say, *"I didn't hear no bell yet."*

Then, one day, she turned the tables on me during tomato canning season. We'd already spent a few days turning basket after basket of tomatoes in sauce or juice or just canned tomatoes that we could eat during the winter. That morning, I woke up exhausted, and my body was aching. (No joke: canning tomatoes is hard work.) Complaining all the way, I was met with the sarcastic reply, *"I didn't hear no bell yet."*

And we kept going because both of us knew what this phrase meant.

- You don't quit until the fight is over.
- Keep going.

- Stop complaining and get back to doing what you're supposed to do.

Did you hear a bell? Then the fight isn't over. We don't give up in the middle of a task just because it's hard or we are tired. Put on your big boy pants and get back in the fight.

This is a wake-up call that today's church needs to hear. Too many men of God are breaking before they hear a bell.

But here's the thing: as followers of Christ, we shouldn't expect to hear any bells. Instead, we should listen for trumpets.

★★★★★★★★★★★★
DID YOU HEAR A BELL? THEN THE FIGHT ISN'T OVER. WE DON'T GIVE UP IN THE MIDDLE OF A TASK JUST BECAUSE IT'S HARD OR WE ARE TIRED. PUT ON YOUR BIG BOY PANTS AND GET BACK IN THE FIGHT.
★★★★★★★★★★★★

1 Thessalonians 4:16-18 says,

> *For the Lord himself will descend from heaven with a cry of command, with the voice of an archangel, and with the sound of the trumpet of God. And the dead in Christ will rise first.*
>
> *Then we who are alive, who are left, will be caught up together with them in the clouds to meet the Lord in the air, and so we will always be with the Lord.*
>
> *Therefore, encourage one another with these words.* (ESV)

These verses talk about the rapture of the church—the day when Jesus will come back to take His followers with Him to Heaven. Notice that the sound of a trumpet will precede it.

When we look at life through the perspective of eternity, we see that this is the end game for believers. We win when we go to Heaven to spend eternity with Jesus.

Until then, our fight continues. Our calling continues.

Part of being an unbreakable man of God means understanding that we are called to continue living for Jesus, living by God's Word, fighting against sin, leading others to Jesus, and disciplining them until we hear a trumpet sound or Jesus calls us home through death.

This is our mission.

We can't give up when hard times come.

We can't become lazy and neglectful in our relationship with God.

We aren't called to be complacent, to make excuses, or to tolerate sin.

We fight to the end for victory!

This reminds me of another great fighter in movies, Steve Rogers, Captain America.

Cap had a saying that he used in a fight, even when he was a scrawny, unsuper-soldiered guy. Beaten, bruised, and knocked down, he would get back on his feet and say, *"I could do this all day!"*[2]

It's Captain America's catchphrase. Whenever I hear it, I think, *"This needs to be the attitude of every unbreakable man of God when he's battling the things that try to defeat him in life."*

It reminds me of Paul's words in Hebrews 12:1-4:

> ***Therefore, since we are surrounded by so great a cloud of witnesses, let us also lay aside every weight, and sin which clings so closely, and let us run with endurance the race that is set before us,***
>
> ***Looking to Jesus, the founder and perfecter of our faith, who for the joy that was set before him endured the cross,***

*despising the shame, and is seated at the right hand of the throne of God.*

*Consider him who endured from sinners such hostility against himself, so that you may not grow weary or fainthearted.*

*In your struggle against sin you have not yet resisted to the point of shedding your blood. (ESV)*

In these verses, Paul challenges us to do all we can to overcome sin in our lives—especially the sins that *"so easily entangle us."* These are the things that stop us from being an unbreakable man.

Paul compares these sins to a *"weight"* that holds us down and keeps us from growing in our relationship with God and running the race God has for us.

The striking thing here is that Paul doesn't say, *"If you feel like it,"* *"If you can get around to it,"* or *"Do the best you can,"* but Paul gets right to the point when he says, **"In your struggle against sin, you have not yet resisted to the point of shedding your blood."**

Can we take a moment and do a collective Joey Lawrence *"Whoa"*[3] at that last statement?

**Guys, we aren't dead yet. We fight until we die, or the trumpet blows, calling us home! We must fight and win.**

I always think about the life of Caleb in the Bible. I LOVE CALEB! Caleb loved God. He lived his life for God and he never lost the heart of an unbreakable man. Even after his success as a spy, even after he stood with Joshua against the entire nation of Israel, and even after he had wandered forty years in the desert for something he didn't do wrong, he kept this attitude. As an old man, he strapped on his sword and went to Joshua with a heart that believed, *"I didn't hear no bell yet. I still don't have my piece of the Promised Land. I am ready to fight and win! I can do this all day! One more round!"* (Joshua 14:6-15)

Caleb wanted victory and God's blessing, so he strapped on his sword and fought to gain victory. But he didn't stop there. He drove out the enemy in the land he wanted to give his daughter (Joshua 15:13-19). He fought the battle so she wouldn't have to face this enemy!

Man of God, you are a new creature in Christ, and because the Holy Spirit lives inside of you, you can fight and overcome the power of sin in your life. Because you have experienced the transforming power of salvation, you don't need to be a weak, wimpy man who is always broken by the same old sins in your life. Instead, with the help of the Holy Spirit living inside of you, you have all you need to fight and overcome any sin in your life. It will be a life-long battle as you try to walk and serve God daily.

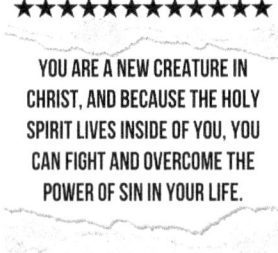

YOU ARE A NEW CREATURE IN CHRIST, AND BECAUSE THE HOLY SPIRIT LIVES INSIDE OF YOU, YOU CAN FIGHT AND OVERCOME THE POWER OF SIN IN YOUR LIFE.

When temptation comes, you can resist.

When you want to fall back into a familiar sin, you don't have to.

Instead, filled with the power of the Holy Spirit and armed with the sword of the Spirit, which is the Word of God, you can stand unbreakable, like Captain America, and say, *"No. I will not lose the battle to sin. I can fight like this all day."*

We can't just give up, lay on the mat, and say, *"It's too hard to be a man of God in today's world. It's too difficult to love my wife and kids—have you met them? Witnessing at work is a struggle—they make fun of me. What's the point anyway?"*

The point is that you are called to something more.

God has a fantastic plan for your life and a purpose that He wants you to fulfill. There are people in your sphere of influence that only you can reach with the Gospel and things that need to be done that only you can do.

Your life has a mission and a purpose. You have a role to play in God's kingdom.

That is why you don't give up. It's why you keep going, trying, praying, reading your Bible, and sharing your testimony until your last breath…or until you hear the trumpet sound. I hope they sound like the trumpets we hear in *Rocky* movies!

Did you hear a trumpet yet? Are you still breathing? Then it's not over. You're not done!

DID YOU HEAR A TRUMPET YET? ARE YOU STILL BREATHING? THEN IT'S NOT OVER. YOU'RE NOT DONE! KEEP GOING. KEEP TRYING. KEEP FIGHTING. KEEP FOLLOWING JESUS.

This might be the end of this book, but it's just the start of your fight!

Keep going. Keep trying. Keep fighting. Keep following Jesus.

As 2 Thessalonians 3:13 says, **"As for you, brothers, do not grow weary in doing good." (ESV)**

Because you didn't hear no bell yet.

You are God's son and an unbreakable man! Keep on Fighting! Make the cry of your heart be, *"I didn't hear no bell yet. I can do this all day, one more round!"*

## Group Study Questions

1. Who would win a fight between Rocky Balboa and Steve Rogers, AKA Captain America?

2. What is the *"bell"* Christians live to hear? What are we called to do until we hear this bell?

3. Why do you think Caleb was able to keep on fighting despite everything he faced in his life? What made him an unbreakable man?

4. This chapter states, *"You are called to something more."* What does this mean? How should it affect your daily life?

5. Are you committed to daily living as an unbreakable man until your last breathe or that trumpet blows?

6. After reading this chapter, what is one thing you will put into practice or one thing you will change in your life?

7. How can we, as a group, help you do this?

# A PERSONAL NOTE FROM JAMIE

Men of God, I want you to remember one thing. I believe in you!

I believe that you have what it takes to walk in your calling as an unbreakable man of God. I believe you have the strength to do whatever God asks of you, to go wherever He leads, and to stand firm against anything and everything the world throws at you. You have what it takes to follow God, to pick up your cross, to follow Him no matter what! God can use you to inspire another man to do the same. You have what it takes!

Nothing can keep you down on the mat. Christ makes you more than conquerors! Victory is promised. It is time for you to get tired of being down on the mat, punch that mat like Donnie Creed did in *Creed II*, get on your feet, and fight like never before. *I didn't hear no bell yet!* Get back in the fight!

*–Jamie Holden*

**UNBREAKABLE**

**Will you accept the challenge of this book?**

If so, state so below:

I, _____ declare today that I will use all of my strength to get up off the mat and get back in the fight. I will obediently follow God as I work to fulfill His purpose for my life. I will overcome whatever personality traits, weaknesses, or hidden sins I have. I will follow God in faith, resolving to stand firm. No matter what the world or the enemy throws at me or what discouragement I face, I will persevere. Even if it brings persecution, I will be grateful to God and wholeheartedly serve Him. I will read and obey His Word, allowing the Bible to convict me and lead me to make changes in my life. God has called me to be an unbreakable man of God, and today, I choose to answer His call!

_____

         Signature                         Date

# WORKBOOK

## Chapter One

Write your definition of *Unbreakable*:

Write your plan for how you will approach this study, i.e., what day/time you will do the reading, etc., so you are prepared for your weekly men's group.

## CONTRACT BETWEEN YOU AND GOD

(And your men's group)

Will you commit to:

Reading each chapter, including Scripture verses?  Yes/No

Sincerely examine your heart using the questions at the end of each chapter?  Yes/No

Openly discussing the chapter with the men in your group with honesty and vulnerability?  Yes/No

I, _____, am committed to getting up off the mat and becoming an unbreakable man living a victorious life. I affirm this decision with my signature.

_____

(Sign)                      (Date)

## Group Study Questions

1. What is your favorite *Rocky* movie?
2. Why do men struggle to get off the mat and gain victory? Why do you?
3. What struggle is constantly beating you down?
4. What have you tried to do to get victory?
5. This chapter quoted Rocky saying, *"If you want to change things in a big way, you need to make some big changes."* Are you willing to make big changes?
6. What does the word *"UNBREAKABLE"* mean to you?
7. After reading this chapter, what is one thing you will put into practice or one thing you will change in your life?
8. How can we, as a group, help you do this?

## Chapter Two

Write down the three types of men discussed in this chapter:

1.

2.

3.

Write down three things you learned from this chapter:

1.

2.

3.

What steps will you take to be a man who is wholeheartedly devoted to God?

**UNBREAKABLE**

## Group Study Questions

1. Who was a better bad guy, Clubber Lang or Ivan Drago?

2. What were the three types of men we discussed in this chapter?

3. Which type of man are you? Be honest with yourself.

4. Why is it so important to recognize and remove our *"high places?"*

5. This chapter stated, *"God allows us to suffer the consequences of not following Him wholeheartedly. He allows us to suffer from our hidden high places, hoping that the suffering will cause us to rip them down and follow Him completely."* How does this passage make you feel?

6. What changes do you need to make to follow God wholeheartedly like David?

7. After reading this chapter, what is one thing you will put into practice or one thing you will change in your life?

8. How can we, as a group, help you do this?

## Chapter Three

This chapter was about choosing WHO you will serve. What is your choice?

What are three changes you will need to make to follow through on this decision.

1.

2.

3.

## Group Study Questions

1. What is your favorite *Rocky* quote?

2. Why is it so hard to reject the world and serve God in our daily lives?

3. What does it really mean to say that you and your house will serve the Lord?

4. Will you serve the world and all it offers, or will you serve the Lord? Honestly think about this choice and decide.

5. Why is it so important for an unbreakable man to make this decision?

6. After reading this chapter, what is one thing you will put into practice or one thing you will change in your life?

7. How can we, as a group, help you do this?

## Chapter Four

What are some areas in which the world has negatively influenced you, causing defeat?   Is freedom worth the fight?

What are three ways you can fight for your freedom?

1.

2.

3.

What are three ways you can stand against evil in today's culture?

1.

2.

3.

## Group Study Questions

1. Why is it so important to remove complacency from our lives?

2. Did the Holy Spirit reveal any areas in your life where you tolerate sin or complacency?

3. How did you respond to the Holy Spirit revealing this sin? What actions did you take?

4. This chapter stated, *"God doesn't want the world to influence us; He wants us to influence the world."* Why does it always seem to end up the other way around? Why are Christians falling into sin instead of standing like a bright light, shining for God in a dark world?

5. Will you remain captive to the sins that so easily control you and the pain of your past, or will you rise like William Wallace and say, *"I want to be free?"*

6. After reading this chapter, what is one thing you will put into practice or one thing you will change in your life?

7. How can we, as a group, help you do this?

## Chapter Five

This chapter discussed the need to discover the weaknesses in our lives that make us vulnerable to sexual sin. What are your weaknesses?

List four practical steps you can take to break free from sexual sin. What can you do differently? What do you need to start doing? What needs to stop?

1.

2.

3.

4.

### UNBREAKABLE

Write down three people you would feel comfortable asking to be an accountability partner.

1.

2.

3.

## Group Study Questions

1. Have you ever played *Madden*? What team do you use?

2. When was the first time you remember seeing pornography? Where were you? How did it happen?

3. This chapter states, "*It is hard to sin sexually while reading the Word of God.*" Why is this true?

4. Which of the eleven points is the one that stood out to you the most?

5. Which one scared you the most?

6. Which one seems impossible to do? Why?

7. Are you willing to once and for all admit your struggle in this area and work to gain victory?

8. After reading this chapter, what is one thing you will put into practice or one thing you will change in your life?

9. How can we, as a group, help you do this?

## Chapter Six

Jeroboam became disappointed with God after being anointed and then having to flee for his life. This disappointment caused him not to trust God's process for success. What disappointments have you faced in life that have weakened your trust and faith in God?


Write down how these disappointments have caused you to fall into sin and be defeated.



Has your life gotten out of balance because you are chasing after success in your own power instead of following God's path? Write down three steps you are going to take to gain balance again:

1.


2.


3.

## Group Study Questions

1. Who are your favorite sports teams?
2. What effect did Jeroboam's being anointed and then having to flee for his life have on his ability to trust God's process?
3. Why do so many men struggle with wanting success?
4. How can chasing success cause us to end up defeated?
5. What is sacrificed in order to gain success?
6. What is keeping you from trusting God to do what He promised?
7. What steps can you take to stop this and become an unbreakable man?
8. After reading this chapter, what is one thing you will put into practice or one thing you will change in your life?
9. How can we, as a group, help you do this?

## Chapter Seven

Do you have any secret sin in your life? What is it?

Think all the way through your secret sin...what could be the consequences of someone else exposing your hidden sins?

In order to break free of secret sin, you need to confess it. Who can you tell your secret sin to so it loses its hold on your life? Who has this sin affected that you need to tell?

Write down three actions you can take to conquer your hidden sin:

1.

2.

3.

## Group Study Questions

1. What does it mean to have unconfessed, hidden sin? Why is it so hard to break free from unconfessed, hidden sin?

2. This chapter stated, *"Whenever we know what the Bible says and choose to do the opposite, we are saying that our sin is more important to us than obeying God."* How does this make you feel?

3. What role does repentance play in overcoming hidden sin? Why is it so difficult? Why is it so important?

4. Why do we believe God is ok with our sins? What does the Bible really say?

5. What was the difference between how Achan and David handled their hidden sin once it was exposed?

6. Will you recognize the damage sin is causing, repent, and partner with the Holy Spirit to do everything necessary to demolish it?

7. After reading this chapter, what is one thing you will put into practice or one thing you will change in your life?

8. How can we, as a group, help you do this?

## Chapter Eight

How did your parents influence your life? Write down your answer.

How would you describe your relationship with your Mom?

How would you describe your relationship with your Dad?

After reading this chapter, what generational patterns have you identified that you need to change?

What are three steps you can take to overcome your generational patterns?

1.

2.

3.

## Group Study Questions

1. What was your relationship with your parents like?

2. How can the way we were raised keep us from becoming unbreakable men?

3. Did the Holy Spirit shine His light on areas you have been following your parent's ways instead of God's ways?

4. What are the signs that we have made a godly parent or mentor an idol?

5. What does the example of the Israelites telling Jesus, *"That's not how our forefathers did it,"* teach us?

6. How can we admire someone's godly character traits without ignoring their flaws and failures?

7. What does it mean to *"Build your own legacy?"*

8. After reading this chapter, what is one thing you will put into practice or one thing you will change in your life?

9. How can we, as a group, help you do this?

## Chapter Nine

What are your triggers, the things that expose your hidden trauma?

What are some steps you can/will take to face and overcome your hidden trauma from your past?

Who do you need to forgive?

What steps will you take to forgive them?

## Group Study Questions

1. As you read through this chapter, did the Holy Spirit bring any areas of trauma or repressed pain to your mind?

2. Do you know of anything that triggers you?

3. How can you use these *"triggers"* as a catalyst for healing and deliverance?

4. How does the the Holy Spirit's role to lead us into truth help us overcome the trauma in our lives?

5. What steps will you take to overcome the repressed pain in your heart?

6. After reading this chapter, what is one thing you will put into practice or one thing you will change in your life?

7. How can we, as a group, help you do this?

## Chapter Ten

Do you tithe? If no, how are you finances doing? If yes, how are you finances being supplied by God?

Do you have a budget? If no, write down the steps you will take to create a budget, ie., who you will ask for help, what you will read, etc.

What appetites did the Holy Spirit reveal to you that affect your financial state? What sucks up your resources?

List five ways you can be a better steward over your finances.

1.

2.

3.


4.


5.


## Group Study Questions

1. Why is financial responsibility an important part of being an unbreakable man?

2. Do you tithe? If so why? If not, why not?

3. What does it mean to be a good steward of the remaining 90%

4. What are some reasons for living on a budget? Do you live on a budget?

5. How do our appetites affect our finances?

6. What is an appetite you have to guard against in order to handle money like a godly man?

7. After reading this chapter, what is one thing you will put into practice or one thing you will change in your life?

8. How can we, as a group, help you do this?

# WORKBOOK

## Chapter Eleven

What are three steps you can take to keep going forward and fighting one more round?

1.

2.

3.

This chapter says you were called to something more. Write down what you think your calling is.

Write down four ways you can defeat sin in your life to become an unbreakable man

1.

2.

3.

4.

**UNBREAKABLE**

## Group Study Questions

1. Who would win a fight between Rocky Balboa and Steve Rogers, AKA Captain America?

2. What is the *"bell"* Christians live to hear? What are we called to do until we hear this bell?

3. Why do you think Caleb was able to keep on fighting despite everything he faced in his life? What made him an unbreakable man?

4. This chapter states, *"You are called to something more."* What does this mean? How should it affect your daily life?

5. Are you committed to daily living as an unbreakable man until your last breathe or that trumpet blows?

6. After reading this chapter, what is one thing you will put into practice or one thing you will change in your life?

7. How can we, as a group, help you do this?

# Bibliography

## Chapter 1

1. *"Box Office MoJo." IMBdPro*, www.boxofficemojo.com/franchise/fr2840039173/. Accessed 11 Sept. 2024.

2. *Creed II*. Directed by Steven Caple JR., performances by Michael B. Jordan and Sylvester Stallone , Metro-Goldwyn-Mayer New Line Cinema, 2018.

## Chapter 2

1. *Rocky III*. Directed by Sylvester Stallone, performances by Sylvester Stallone and Talia Shire, MGM/UA Entertainment Co., 1982.

## Chapter 3

1. *Rocky Balboa*. Directed by Sylvester Stallone, performances by Sylvester Stallone and Burt Young , MGM Distribution Co. (United States) 20th Century Fox (International), 2006.

## Chapter 4

1. *Rocky III*. Directed by Sylvester Stallone, performances by Sylvester Stallone and Talia Shire , MGM/UA Entertainment Co., 1982.

2. *Braveheart*. Directed by Mel Gibson, performances by Mel Gibson and Sophie Marceau, Paramount Pictures (United States and Canada) 20th Century Fox (International), 1995.

## Chapter 8

1. *Rocky III.* Directed by Sylvester Stallone, performances by Sylvester Stallone and Talia Shire , MGM/UA Entertainment Co., 1982.

2. Donald C Stamps, *Study Notes on Romans 8:14, Fire Bible: English Standard Version,* (Peabody, MA: Hendrickson Publishers Marketing, LLC, 2014), Pg 1903.

3. *Creed.* Directed by Ryan Coogler, performances by Michael B. Jordan and Sylvester Stallone, Metro-Goldwyn-Mayer Pictures New Line Cinema Chartoff-Winkler Productions, 2015.

## Chapter 9

1. Weber, Laverne, and Heidi Gregory. *Victory's Journey: Leaders Manual.* Victory's Journey, 2010. pp. 65-67.

2. Weber, Laverne, and Heidi Gregory. *Victory's Journey: Leaders Manual.* Victory's Journey, 2010. pp. 67.

## Chapter 11

1. *Rocky V.* Directed by John G. Avildsen, performances by Sylvester Stallone and Talia Shire , MGM/UA Entertainment Co., 1990.

2. *Captain America: The First Avenger.* Directed by Joe Johnston, performances by Chris Evans and Tommy L. Jones, Paramount Pictures, 2011.

3. "Blossom: Joey's "Whoa!" Catchphrase On 'Was From The TV Icon Gods' | *PeopleTV.*" Youtube, uploaded by Peopel, 11 Oct. 2017, youtu.be/wz66Cq Hh-Q?si=nQ8getAvP-NaVuty.

# Also Available

### VICTORY IS AVAILABLE TO YOU. THROUGH GOD
## YOU ARE UNBREAKABLE!

Put your faith into action with this year-long Bible reading plan designed to help you become an unbreakable man of God!

VISIT WWW.MANTOURMINISTRIES.COM//BIBLEPLAN

## ALSO AVAILABLE FROM MANTOUR MINISTRIES

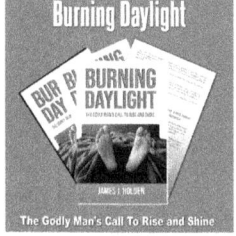

**Available in print and digital formats.
Visit www.mantourministries.com
for more information.**

Jamie loves to speak to men and is available to speak at your next men's event. Jamie combines humor and his personal testimony to engage and challenge men to grow in their walk with God. He uses his testimony of overcoming abuse and dealing with his physical and emotional issues growing up to encourage men that no matter what their background or where they have come from in life, they can grow into mighty men in God's kingdom.

"Years ago, while I was attending the University of Valley Forge, God gave me a deep desire to minister to men. My calling is to help men learn what it means to be a godly man and how to develop a deep, personal relationship with their heavenly Father. We strive to challenge and encourage men to reach their full potential in God's kingdom."

If you are interested in having Jamie at your next men's event as a speaker or workshop leader, or if you are interested in having him come share with your church, contact him by visiting www.mantourministries.com/invitejamie. He is also available to speak for one or multiple weeks on the theme of his books.

www.ingramcontent.com/pod-product-compliance
Lightning Source LLC
Chambersburg PA
CBHW050909160426
43194CB00011B/2336